BALLAD OF A THIN MAN:

In Search of Ryan Larkin

By Chris Robinson

Illustrations by Theodore Ushev

AWN PRESS

President and Co-Publisher, AWN Press: Ron Diamond
COO and Co-Publisher, AWN Press: Dan Sarto
Senior Book Editor, AWN Press: Jon Hofferman

Publisher and General Manager, Thomson Course Technology PTR: Stacy L. Hiquet
Associate Director of Marketing: Sarah Panella
Manager of Editorial Services: Heather Talbot
Marketing Manager: Jordan Casey
Executive Editor: Kevin Harreld
Editorial Services Coordinator: Jen Blaney
DVD Producer: Brandon Penticuff

ISBN-10: 1-59863-560-3
ISBN-13: 978-1-59863-560-7

Library of Congress Catalog Card Number: 2008936198
Printed in Canada
1 2 3 4 5 6 7 11 10 09

Front cover design by Svetla Protitch.

AWN Press
A division of AWN, Inc.
6525 Sunset Blvd., GS 10
Los Angeles, CA 90028
http://www.awn.com

Course Technology
25 Thomson Place
Boston, MA 02210
www.courseptr.com

For Jarvis Robinson Neall

He is searching for himself. He is not ready to entertain such a notion, because like the rest of us he seeks an eternal saviour.

– Philip K. Dick, *Valis*

Little boy lost, he takes himself so seriously.

– Bob Dylan, "Visions of Johanna"

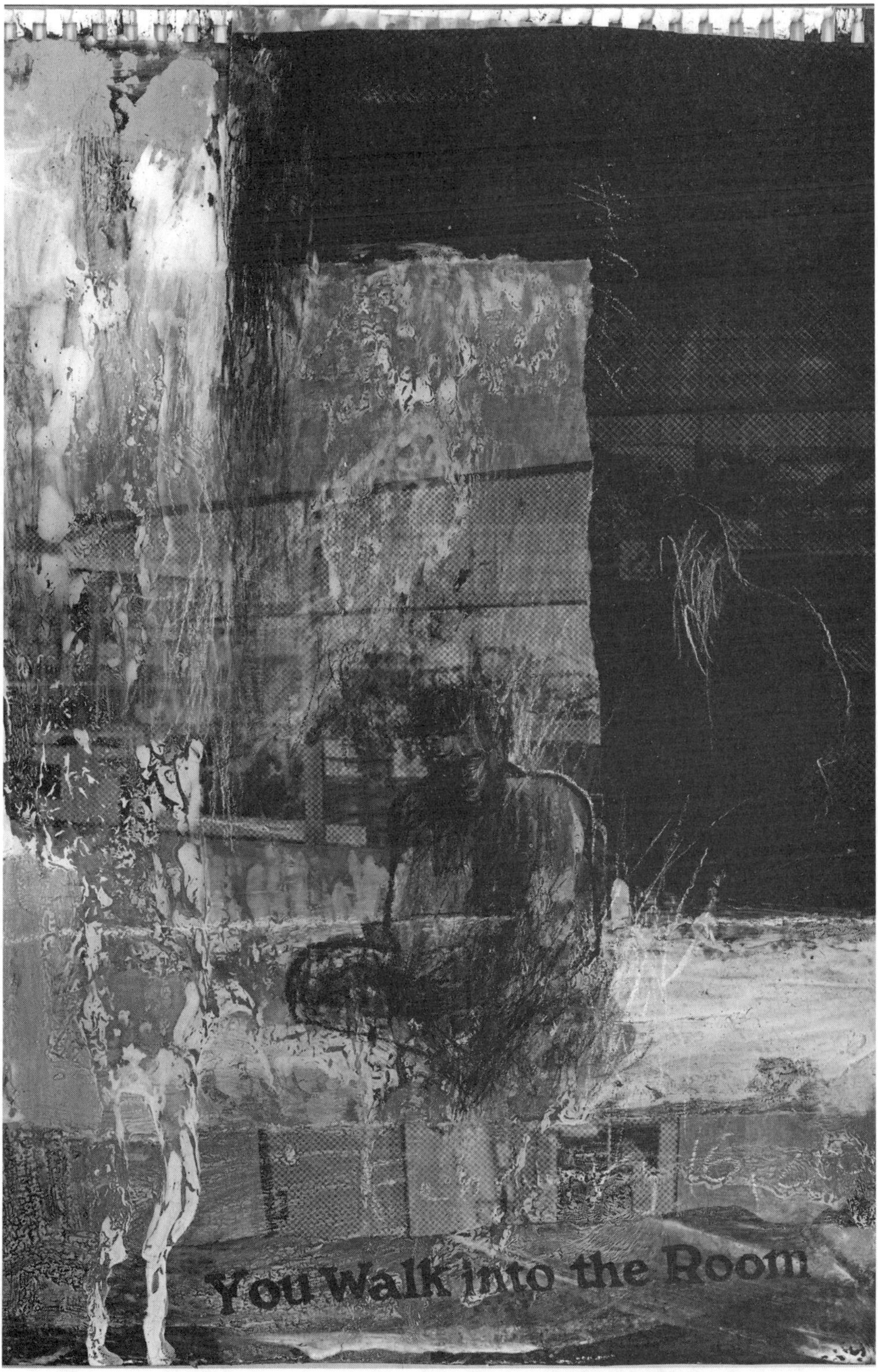
You Walk into the Room

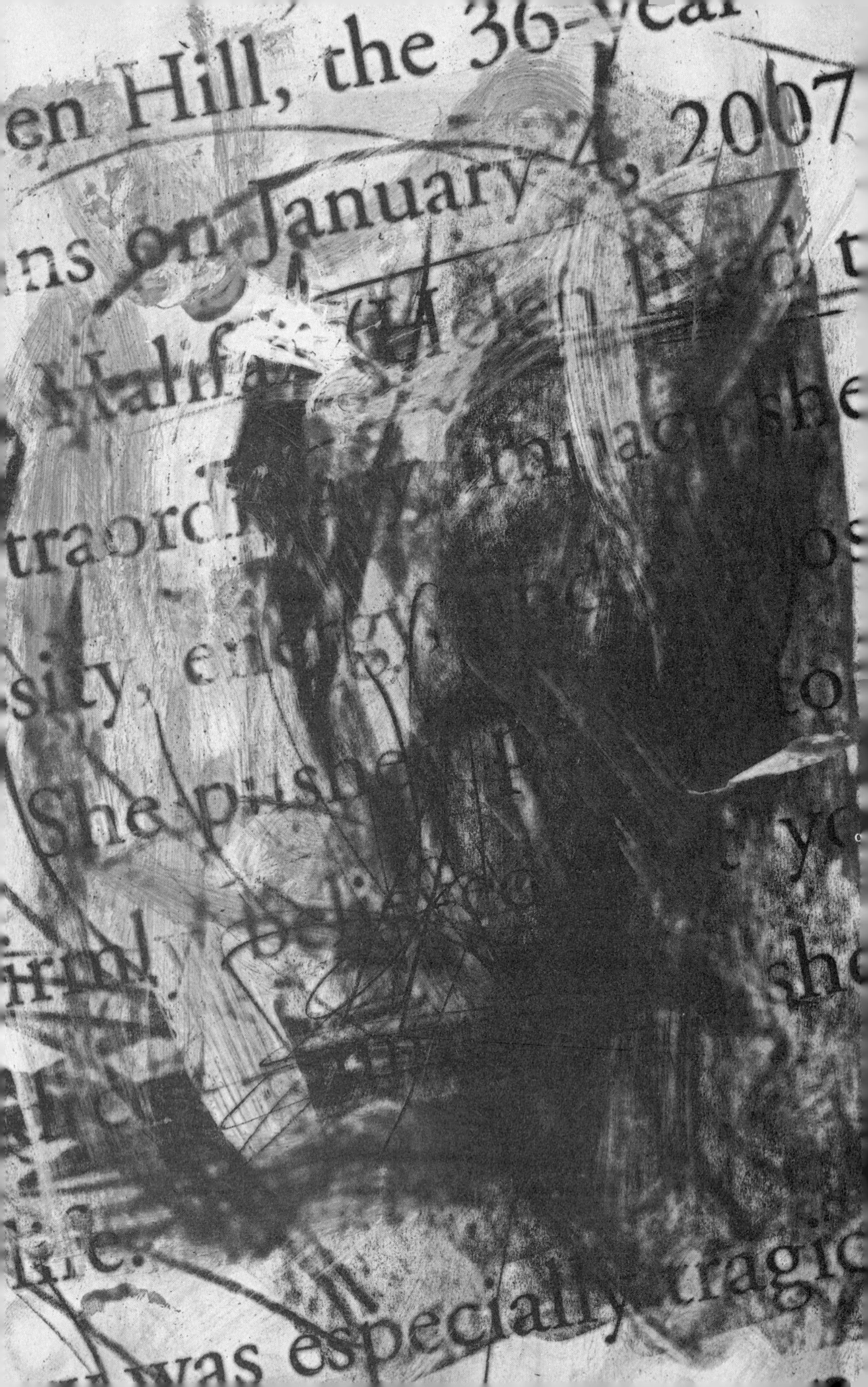
en Hill, the 36-year
ns on January
2007
sity
She
was especially tragic

February 16, 2008. Halifax airport. Floor.

I'm early for my flight home. I sit on the floor and check my email. There's a message telling me that Montreal animator Ryan Larkin died two days ago on February 14, 2007.

I had very mixed feelings about Ryan's passing. I cringed at the thought that the hyperbole ("genius," "tragedy") would be tossed around freely by those who didn't know him. Ryan Larkin was not an artistic genius. He made four films, all of which showed great promise, but, with the exception of *Walking*, you'd be hard pressed to call any a masterpiece. His films were rambling and incomplete, a bit like his life.

I thought about the life of Helen Hill, the 36-year-old animator who was murdered in New Orleans on January 4, 2007. The night Ryan died I was at a screening in Halifax (Helen lived there for five years) and saw firsthand the extraordinary impact she had on the arts community. Helen's generosity, energy, and explosive optimism literally changed people's lives. She pushed people to be better. She didn't make excuses. Helen firmly believed that you had to take responsibility for your life and community. In a short time, Helen squeezed every breath out of life.

In this context, Ryan's story was especially tragic. Ryan was given a relatively long life and wasted innumerable opportunities to turn his life around. There were always fears and excuses. When he did finally appear to be turning a corner, life finally said, sorry bud, it's too late.

As different as their lives were, though, Ryan's life, like Helen's, had an impact on many people.

I was one of them.

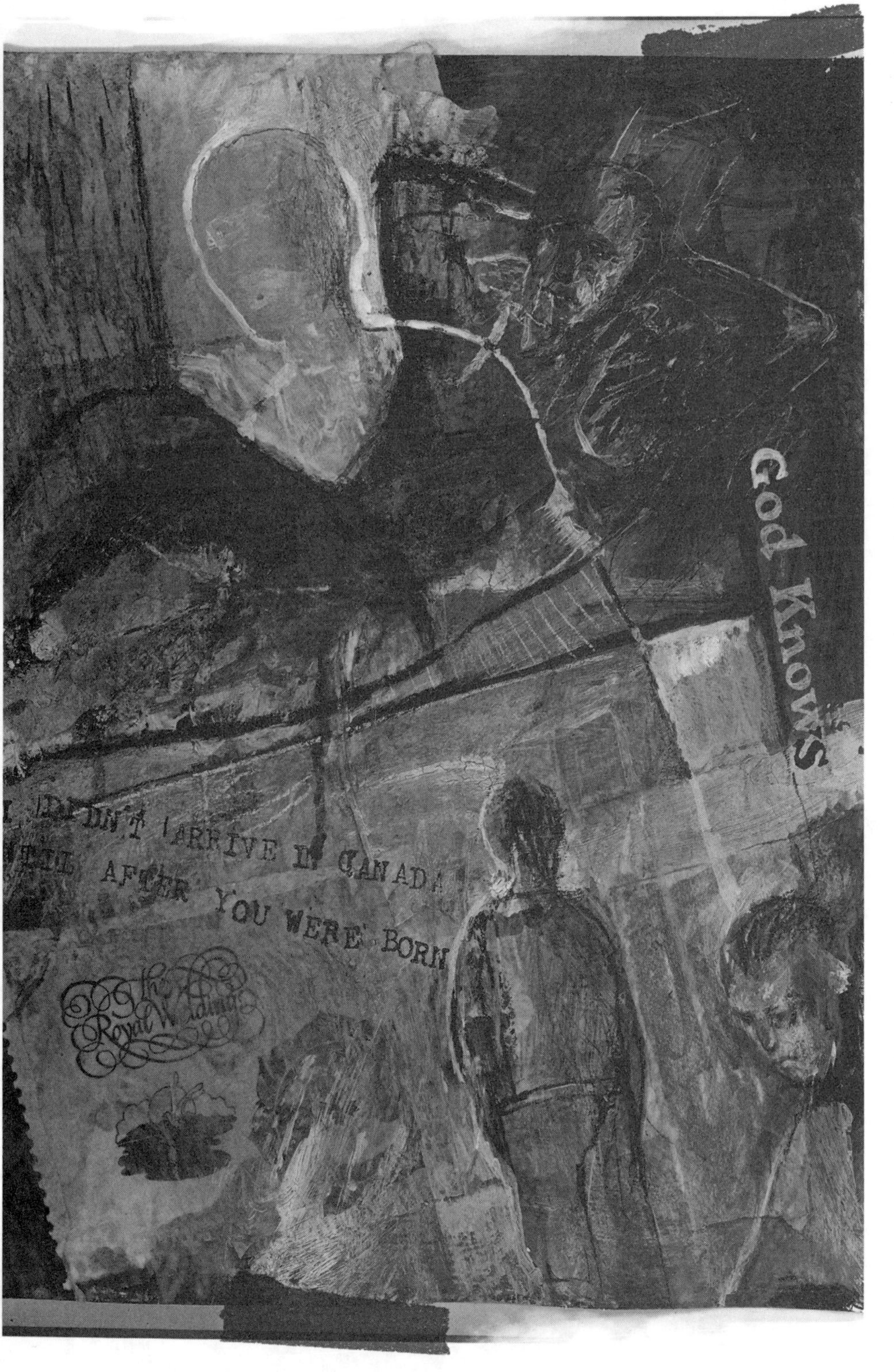
God Knows
DIDN'T ARRIVE IN CANADA
AFTER YOU WERE BORN
The Royal Wedding

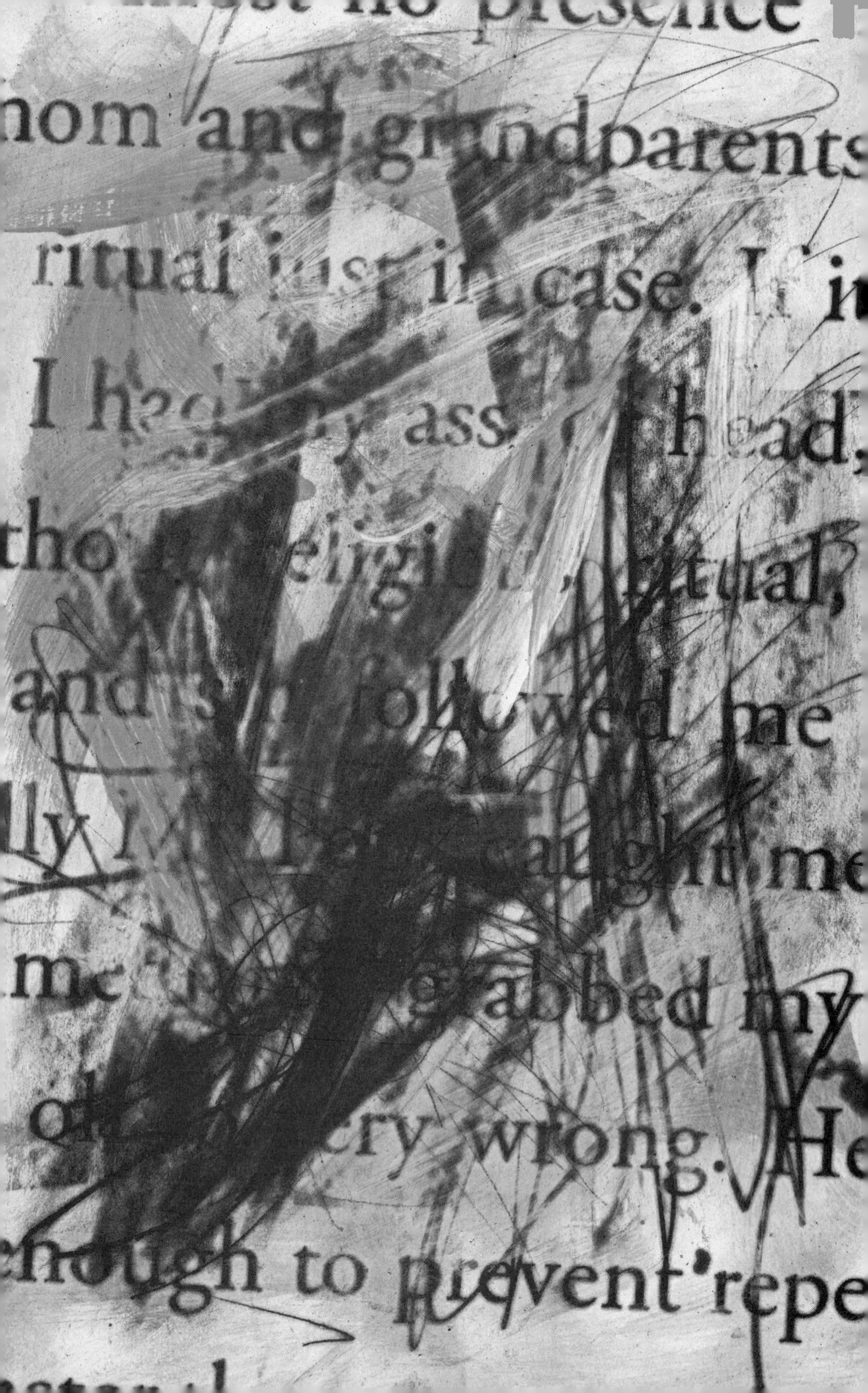
nom and grandparents
ritual in case.
ass head,
tho ritual,
and followed me
lly aught me
grabbed my
ery wrong. He
nough to prevent repe

I was born Anglican, but my family never went to church and religion had almost no presence in our home. I was baptized, but I figure my mom and grandparents (who were also raising me) went through the ritual just in case. If it turned out that there was a God, then at least I had my ass, or head, covered.

Even without religious ritual, the suspiration of heaven, hell, God, devil, and sin followed me with airless gloom. When I was six, Not Really My Pops caught me in bed with my hands down my pants. He immediately grabbed my hand, pulled it away and told me that this was oh so very wrong. He didn't explain why and, well, it wasn't quite enough to prevent repeat visits for the next 34 years.

During Easter that same year, he bought me *The Bible for Children*. It was a strange gift, but in hindsight made a lot more sense than tossing me chocolates. I suspect that the gift was also motivated by my bodily crime, as though Not Really My Pops was telling me, "See, this is what happens to those who fondle themselves." Inside this picture Bible I came across a story that I've never forgotten. In search of the newly born Jesus, King Herod, frustrated by his inability to find the baby, orders his soldiers to go into Bethlehem and slaughter all the babies. Accompanying the story is a vivid picture of ferocious-faced soldiers ripping babies from the arms of their horrified mothers. In the background lay dead babies. The scene horrified me and gave me nightmares for days. Was this what God, Jesus and heaven were about? Is this what happened to kids who touched themselves? Is this sin?

The third and most vivid encounter occurred in my early teens. I'd returned from a Montreal Expos baseball game with a friend and her family. They were likeable, but rather intense religious types. While settling down to crash at their place for the night, I asked my friend about this heaven and hell business. I don't remember specifics about the conversation except that her description of hell scared the shit out of me and to this day lingers in my consciousness. She told me about fires and demons and eternal suffering.

While these events left me with an imprint of suffocating guilt, they never quite scared me straight. Throughout my youth, I stole, fought, fucked and, yes, even continued to touch myself. I was a reluctant sinner, swirling in a maelstrom of purgatory, unable to commit myself to either heaven or hell. Being angelic was dull and Hell was frightening.

I think I now understand why these images terrified me. Having been conceived by two strangers, life has always felt very tenuous and fragile to me. My childhood existence was one of continual emotional death. I had parents who didn't want me. Biopops refused to accept responsibility and fled the country. My mother, being too young to raise me, gladly let my grandmother become my surrogate. She was my saint, angel, and savior; a loving, kind woman who was even going to adopt me when my mother decided she didn't want to keep me. Why my mother changed her mind about giving me up is beyond me. Maybe she figured she'd learn to love me. Her thanks to my grandmother for caring and loving me was to take me away from her. Then she scurried around trying to find a man to marry. Eventually, she found one, a guy she met at a party. They married soon after. It was a match made in Hell. When they weren't ignoring, chastising or swatting me, they drove each other towards violence and bouts of madness.

I was swallowed up by this world of hate and I lashed out at the world around me, creating a tornado of hate, violence and pain. I wanted everyone to suffer my suffering.

At 15, there was a small light. Not Really My Pops calls me into his bedroom. He's lying on the bed, legs apart, hands resting behind his head. He looks smug and macho. I figured I'd done something wrong again. The usual interrogation began, but the first question surprised me. "When did I come to Canada?" A strange question, I thought. I tell him I don't know, that I figure he arrived a year before I was born.

"Nope," he says.

After a long period of awkward silence he continues with this annoying game. "I didn't arrive in Canada until after you were born."

I didn't expect this. I had recently figured out that they got married a few years after I was born, but I never suspected that this man wasn't my father.

I was stunned and relieved. I didn't really like Not Really My Pops (as I now called him in my mind) much. Sure, he was okay sometimes. Helped out with sports, but mostly I was scared of him. He had little patience and was never pleased with my efforts. When my friends came over, he regularly assaulted them with sarcasm and put-downs. He thought it was charming or cool, that it would appeal to kids. He was wrong. They thought he was an ass. Soon, most kids didn't want to come to my house anymore.

Despite the revelation, no one will tell me anything about Biopops. Not Really My Pops knows nothing about the man, and my mother won't discuss the issue.

My life changed with this news. I descended deeper into my own hell. Like Dante, I had to stumble and fall before I arose to touch the stars. Biopops became my Beatrice. He would redeem me and carry me out of this God-forsaken mess that was my "family."

I had been in search of a saviour ever since my grandmother was taken from me. I looked for salvation everywhere, through hockey cards, hockey players, sports, booze, sex, fights; anyone or anything that would make me feel. I was alive but moving without life. I had no sense of who I was or what I wanted. I hated (like many people) being asked by teachers what I wanted to do with my life, or where I saw myself in five years. I had no answer. I didn't know where I was now, how could I know where I'd be then?

The truth about my father freed me, but not in a good way. The house became a hotel. Everyone just came and went at will with little contact. There were no shared dinners. Mother was cloistered in the basement watching television. My room became a refuge. Except for food and laundry, I have little reason to leave it. I turned myself into a martyr. More than ever, I had no reason to be afraid of or concerned about my non-parents. I didn't have to listen to them. The fear I felt for Not Really My Pops was replaced by contempt. I became increasingly distant, ignored curfews, neglected school, drank more, shoplifted, and got into more fights and arguments at home. I became the devil.

I often dreamt about Biopops. Was he rich? Was he happy? I often imagined –like most in that position—that Biopops lived in a big white house with large windows and a yard. The sun always shone. There were regular family gatherings with lots of food, drink and laughs. It was Heaven.

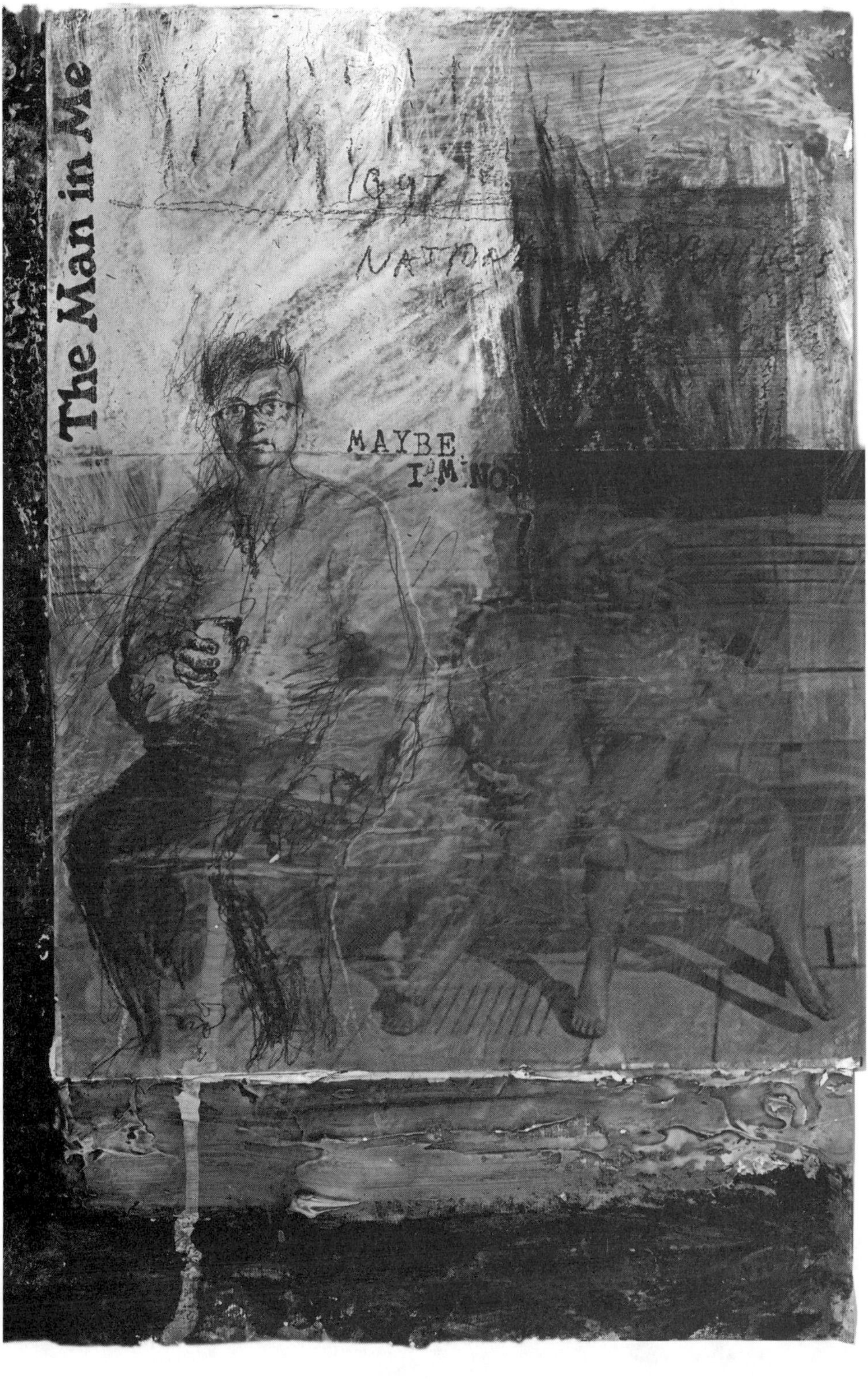
The Man in Me
1997
MAYBE

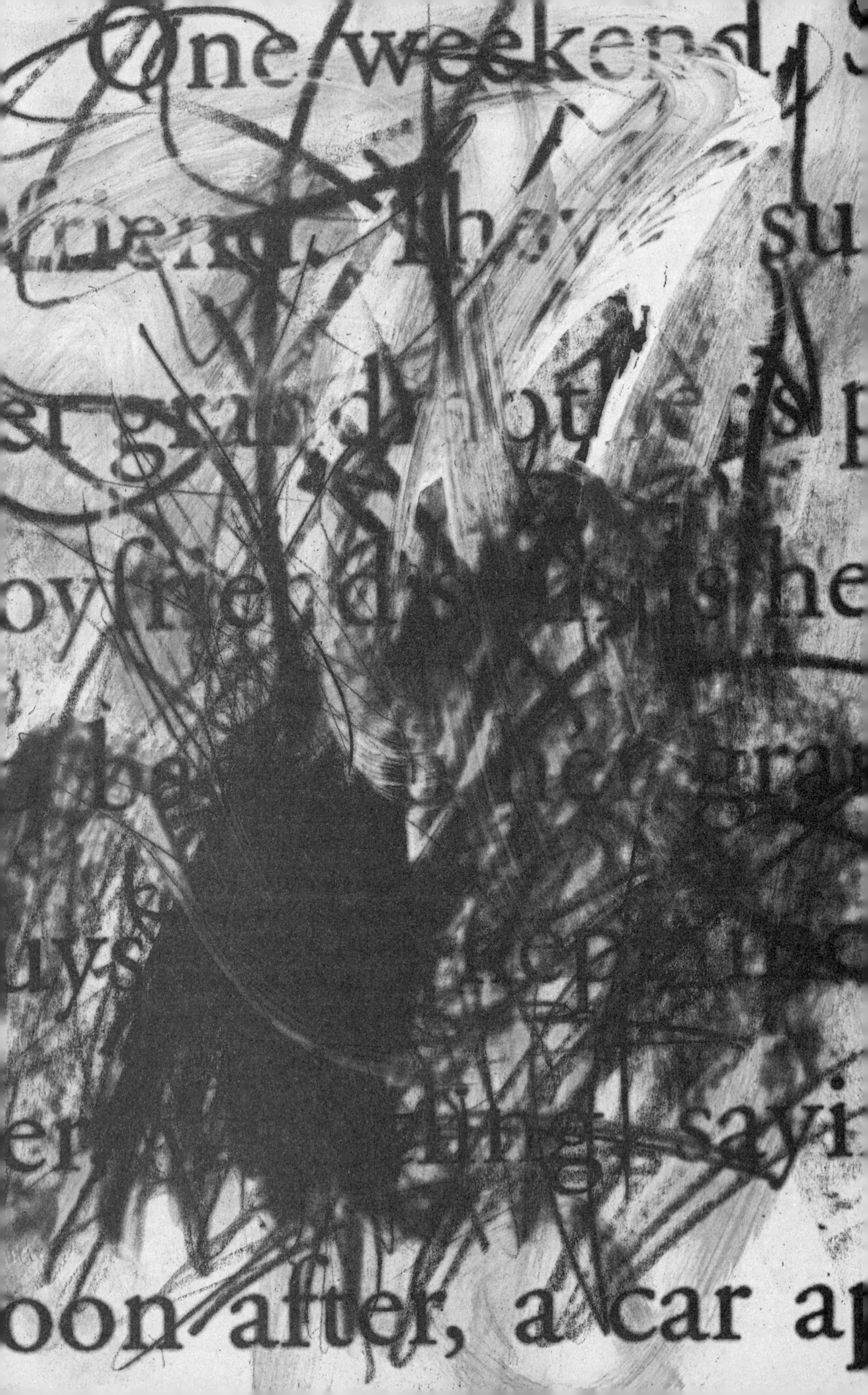

One weekend
su
er grand
oyfriend
he
ays
ing sayi
oon after, a car ap

One weekend. September 1966. My mother is in Toronto with a friend. They're supposed to go to a party and then she's staying at her grandmother's place for the weekend. Things go wrong when her boyfriend stands her up. She hurt. While waiting at a subway stop to go back to her grandmother's place alone, she was hassled by some guys. She kept moving away from them, but they kept following her, whistling, saying lewd things: "Whatcha got under that skirt?" Soon after, a car approached. A man rolled down the window and asked her if she was okay. She said, yes. He offered her a drive. She accepted. They exchanged a few pleasantries in the car. He said that he was getting ready to go back to school in Detroit. His parents lived in North York so her grandmother's place was on the way. She invites him in. Figures what the hell, her weekend has been ruined already. They drink and have sex. Lucky if they spent a few hours together.

When she learned she was pregnant, my mother took a train back to Toronto with my grandmother. She had written down the man's address before he left that night. She decided to go alone. His mother answered the door. My mother nervously explained the situation. The woman responded in anger. Asked her how she knew it was her son. Didn't she have a steady boyfriend before that? How did she know it wasn't him? In the end, she told Mother to go away and closed the door.

Heartbreaking stuff.

I didn't find any of this out until much later. It wasn't until I was about 18 that I even learned his name. Then it took a few more years and a night of drinks to pry more information out of her.

Most days I didn't care. Then came the binge period where nothing was more pressing than finding and knowing my father.

But I kinda like the imagining part. That way my Biopops could be anyone I wanted him to be. Maybe he was somehow connected to

Pete Townshend? That would explain my obsession with The Who and Townshend's angry songs about identity.

In 1997, I made a visit to the National Archives in Ottawa. I didn't know where to start, but was finally led to check the city directories. These proto phonebooks not only listed phone numbers, but they listed the occupants of every residence. The last name was fairly common so I had to photocopy dozens of pages. For whatever reason, I decided to stop after I got the photocopies. I put them away and forgot the matter again.

Two years later, while searching in the basement for something else, I saw the directory pages again. I pulled them out and had a glance. Incredibly, within minutes, I was certain that I'd found the right address. Now, the directory was for 1966, so there was no guarantee that anyone still lived there, but I was almost certain that I'd located my Biopops' Toronto home.

A day later I'd found a number for a man I was sure was my Biograndpops. I was too nervous and scared to call so my wife Kelly did it for me. Sure enough, he was Biopops' father. He had Biopops' number in Detroit but said that he wasn't there, he was at the family cottage near Peterborough. He didn't have that number though. Said we should call Biopop's brother.

I was stunned at how easy it was. "Can you believe this?" I said to Kelly. "In a matter of minutes, we've tracked down the man who might be my real father."

My wife called his brother and he readily – to my surprise – gave her the number for the family's cottage.

The next day I was sitting in the office. I held the phone in one hand and with shaking hands dialed the cottage number. "What am I gonna say? What if he is angry and hangs up?" Maybe he's not ready for this. Maybe I'm not.

Fortunately there was no answer.

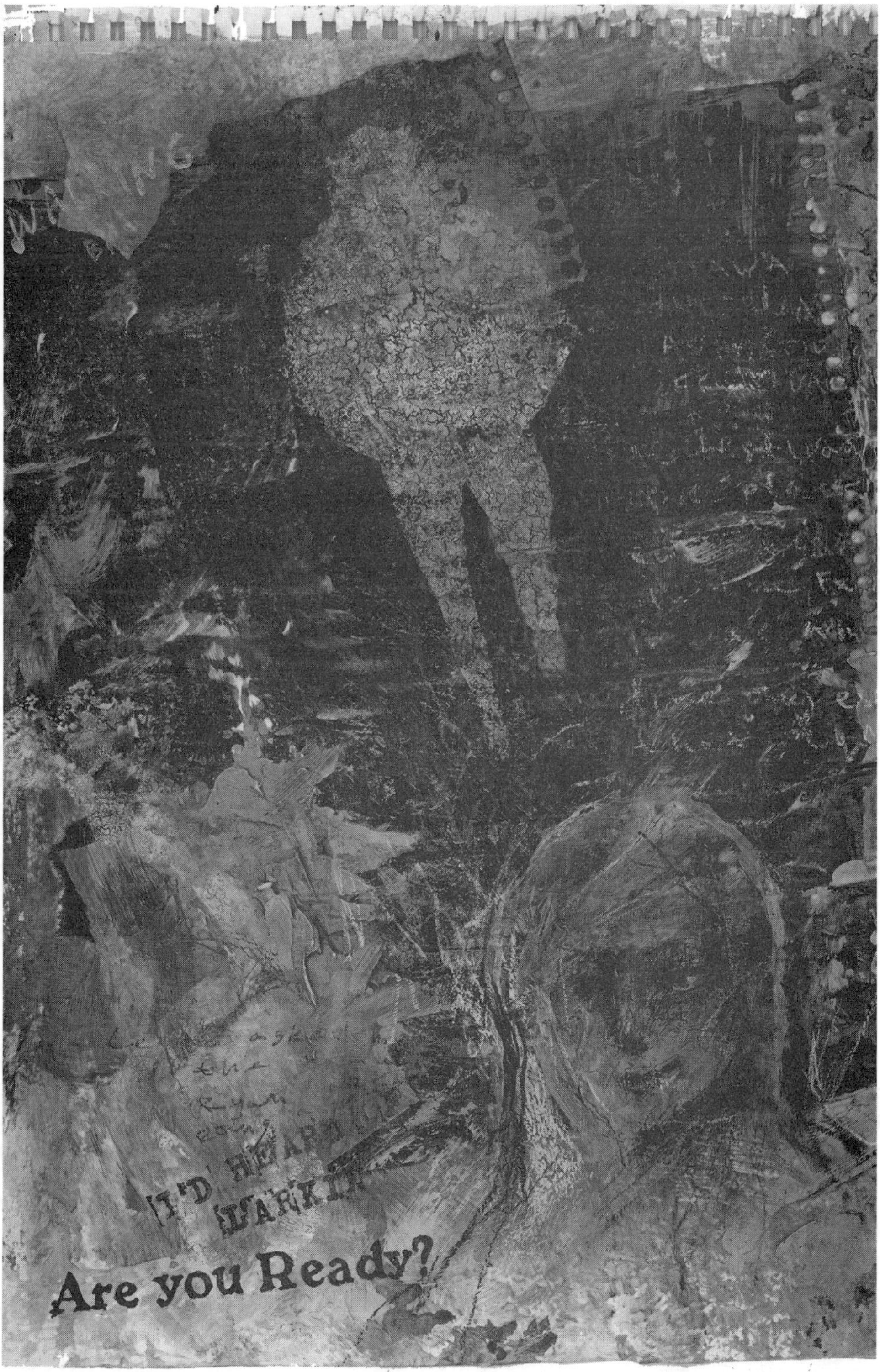
Are you Ready?

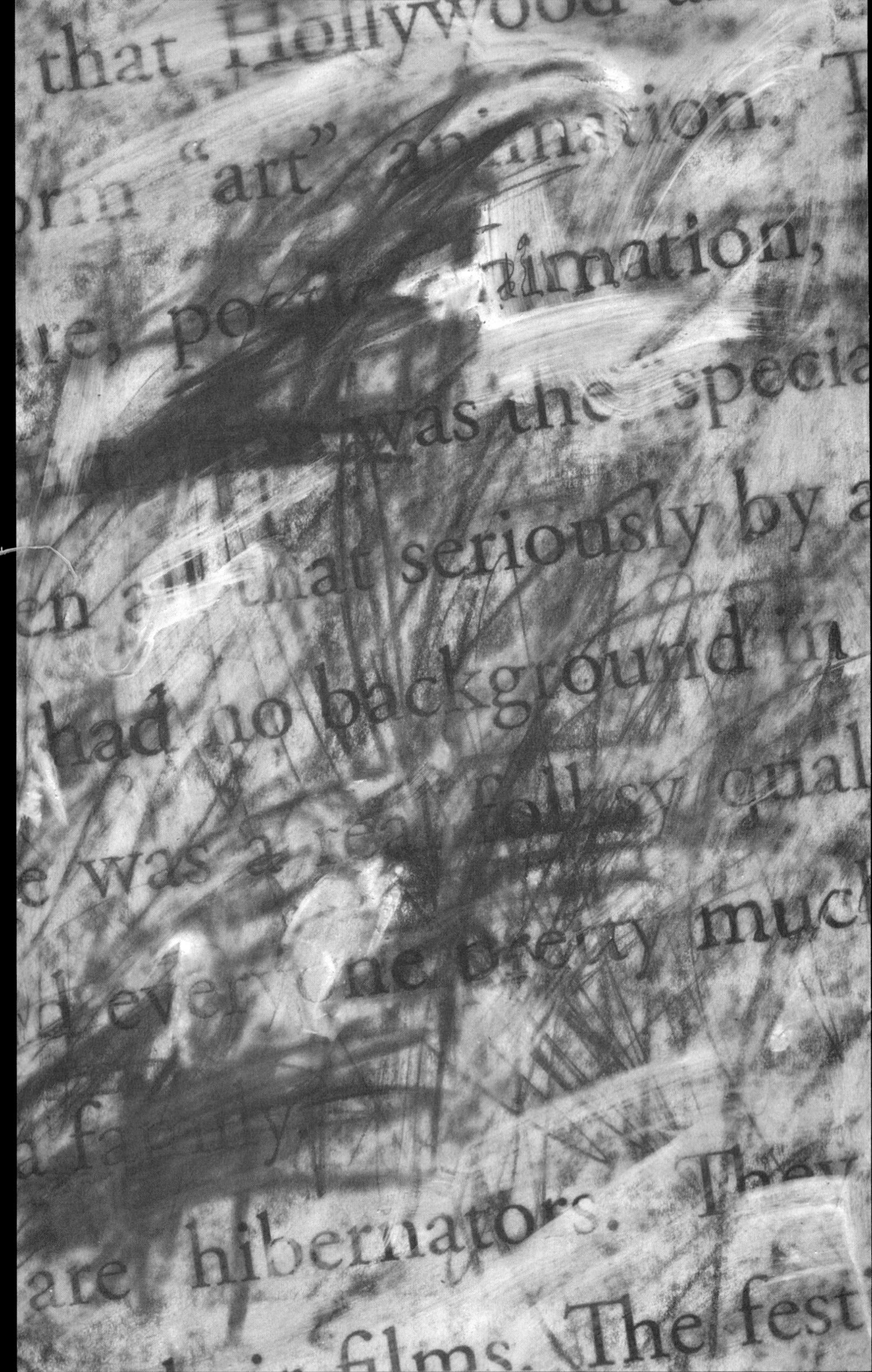
that Hollywood
"art" animation
mation,
was the specia
seriously by a
had no background
was a
qual
much
hibernators. They
films. The fest

The Ottawa International Animation Festival is located in an old stone courthouse in the city's downtown. In 1988, it was renovated and turned into a building for arts groups. I'd been working for the festival since 1991 and had taken over as director in 1995. I'd recently given up my role as executive director. Kelly, eager to get out of the house and with our son Jarvis now old enough to stay with his grandma, came back to the festival (she had previously worked on the 1994 festival) and took over as managing director. I remained as the artistic director. The previous years had made it clear that I was not fit for, or even interested in, running the festival. Aside from the drinking, I was having panic attacks, explosive manic tendencies, and just couldn't do the job I was supposed to do. So I said fuck it, gave up the "throne," and concentrated on writing, programming, and sorting my shit out.

The festival took place every year in the fall. It was a massive five-day event that required a year of planning and preparation. We're fortunate in one sense to have taken on a festival with a long history and good reputation. It was also the only major animation festival in North America, so we attracted a lot of Canadians and Americans. Still, it was a tough sell because we weren't peddling kiddie animation or the usual drivel that Hollywood and TV churn out. We were promoting short-form "art" animation. There wasn't much of an audience for mature, poetic animation, since most people didn't know it existed. Animation was the "special cousin" in the film world and not really taken all that seriously by anyone except those within the community. I had no background in animation but I really liked the people. There was a real folksy quality to everyone. There were very few egos and everyone pretty much knew everyone else. It was very much like a family.

Animators are hibernators. They spend their year working, mostly alone, on their films. The festival, even if they don't have a film showing, is their one chance a year to get out and meet their old friends, see new films, and just relax with people of their ilk.

With the exception of Kelly and me, the bulk of the staff were hired on a short-term basis between May and September. Most of them were, as I'd been, university grads who had no idea what they wanted out of life. The festival was a temporary place for most of our employees. They considered us a pit stop before they went back into the race. They just didn't seem to care that for Kelly and me, this was the race.

One of the exceptions at that time was a staff member named Lesya. She'd started out as a volunteer. When we saw that she was more reliable and responsible than most of the paid staff, we hired her back the next year. I also really liked her. She was quirky, but in a loveable sense. Sort of reminded me of Perini Scleroso, Andrea Martin's immigrant cleaning woman character on SCTV. Lesya, although she was a descendent of Poles and Ukrainians, spoke English fine, but like Scleroso, she was always happy. It wasn't strange to see Lesya singing some crazy song aloud in the office or just murmuring to herself. She brought so much good energy to the office.

Sometime in June 2000, Lesya came up to me all giddy. She'd spent the weekend in Montreal visiting a friend. Her friend worked at a restaurant on St. Laurent Street called Schwartz's. She told Lesya that apparently an old animator panhandles outside the restaurant every day. Lesya then asked me if the name Ryan Larkin rang a bell.

I'd heard of Larkin. I'd read a passage in a book on Canadian animation that said he got into drugs and alcohol and at one point was getting his government paycheques (he worked for the National Film Board of Canada, the country's film studio) sent to his house in a taxicab. I knew his film *Walking* was considered a masterpiece of animation. Personally, I thought *Walking* was just some crazy hippie shit from the sixties.

And that was all I'd ever thought of Ryan Larkin.

But after hearing Lesya's story, suddenly I was thinking a lot about Larkin. I wondered if anyone had ever tried to help him. It seemed strange that a guy who was apparently a pretty talented animator could have fallen so hard. I figured there might be a pretty intriguing story behind his apparent crash. Maybe we could also help him. Perhaps all he needed was someone to give him a hand. It all happened so fast. In a flash, I became obsessed with finding out if this was Ryan Larkin and if there was something we could do to save him.

Without really knowing what we could do, let alone whether Larkin even wanted or needed any help, Lesya and I drove to Montreal the next day to find Ryan.

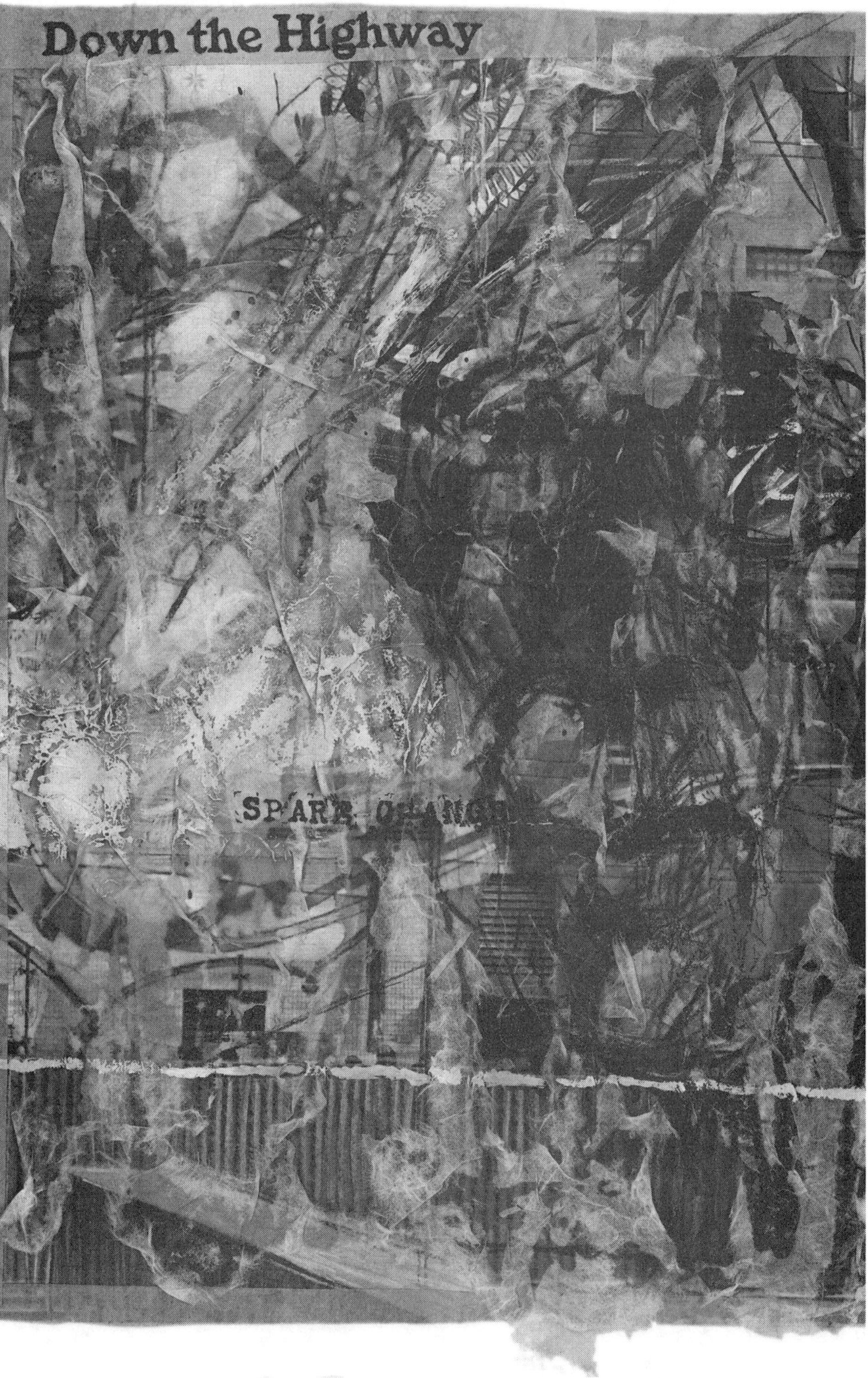
Down the Highway

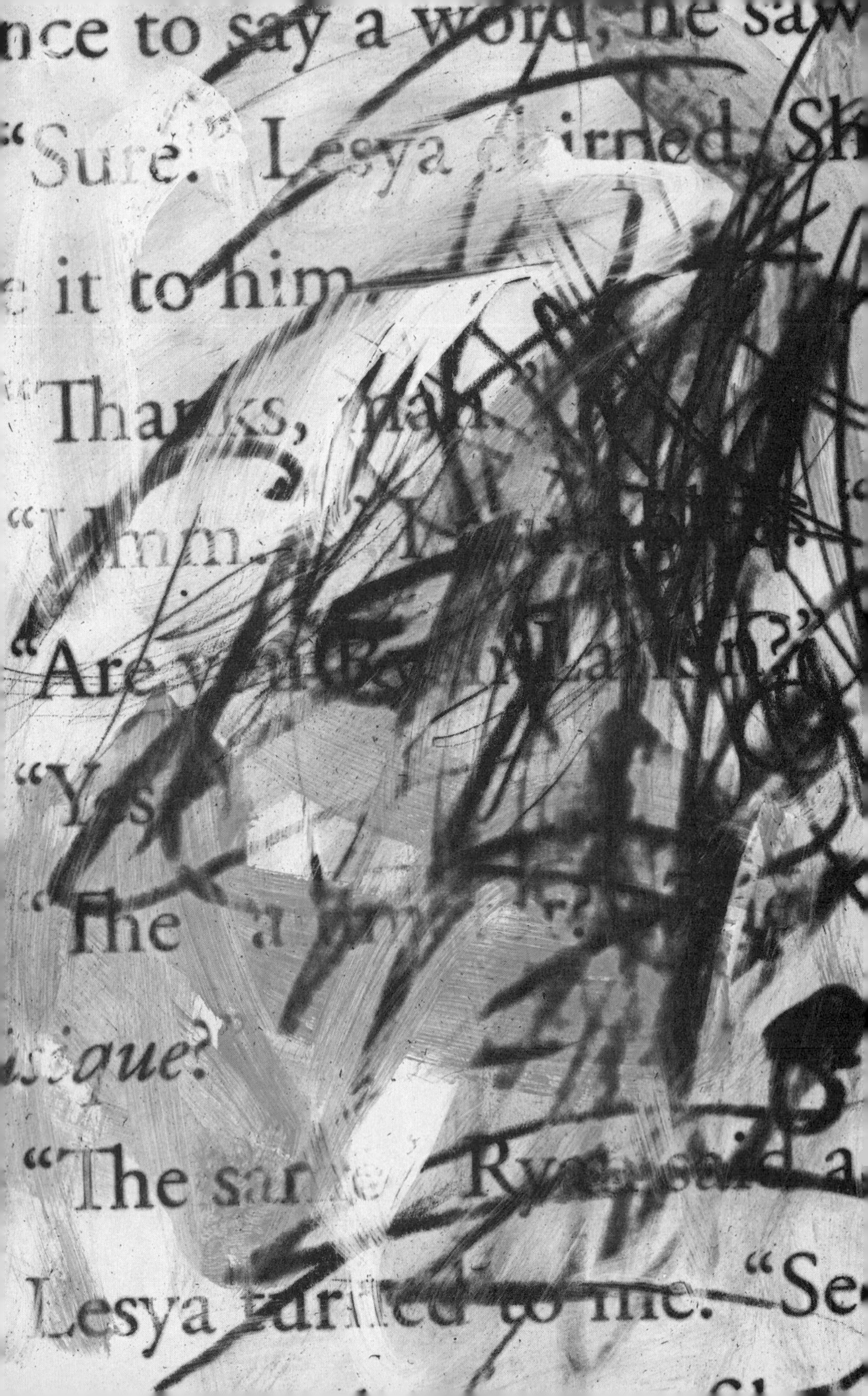
nce to say a word, he saw
"Sure." Lesya
it to him
"Tha
"Are
"The
isque?
"The sa
Lesya
"Se

We left the office early. During the drive to Montreal, we talked about what we were going to do once we got there. There was always a chance that it wouldn't be Larkin. If not, then we'd just go out and get drunk. At least, I would. If it was Larkin, the plan was that we'd invite him out for a drink/dinner and then see what unfolds from there. I was a bit nervous. I had no idea what we could offer this guy. Maybe it was a good excuse to get ripped with someone. I dunno.

It took us about two hours to get to Montreal. We found a parking spot just off St. Laurent and headed up the street in search of this mysterious hobo. It didn't take us long to find the guy. He was sitting on a concrete block in front of a chainlink fence. The man was a real mess. He was seated on a bench. He had a smoke in his right hand. It shook as he brought it to his trembling lips. He must have been about 60, but he was trying to look half that. His wig and eyebrows were dyed jet black. He wore a T-shirt. He was a small, fragile man. Looked like you could blow him over with a breath. Before we had a chance to say a word, he saw us and said, "Spare change?"

"Sure!" Lesya chirped. She grabbed a loonie from her pocket and gave it to him.

"Thanks, man."

"Umm…" I mumbled. "I don't want to bother you… but…"

"Are you Ryan Larkin?" Lesya cut in.

"Yes."

"The animator? The guy who made *Walking* and *Street Musique*?"

"The same," Ryan said as he stood up and bowed to us.

Lesya turned to me. "See, I told you."

"Do you know my films?"

"Well, I know of them. I've never seen them," Lesya said. "My friend Erin works at Schwartz's Deli. She told me about you."

"She's a charming young lady. Always very kind to me."

"Well, it's nice to meet you," I said, suddenly regretting this whole trip. "We should probably let you get back to your, umm, work."

"Have you eaten?" Lesya suddenly said.

"I'm not really that hungry. I'll get some chicken wings later."

"Why don't you come out for some beers with us?"

"Lesya, I'm sure Ryan has other stuff to do."

"Yeah… I'm working right now. I can't afford to lose my salary, man."

"Well," said Lesya, "how much do you normally make during a shift?"

"About $40-50."

"Well, what if we give you $50 and take you for beer and wings?"

"Lesya…" I said, embarrassed.

"Come on, Chris," she whispered to me. "Aren't you at least curious to find out his story?"

"Fine." I pulled out two twenties and a ten and handed them to Ryan.

"Thanks, man. That's great. Fantastic. Really." His quivering hand placed the bills in his pant pocket.

"Well, let's go."

"Okay… just let me get my things."

Ryan had a small plastic pop bottle, a gym bag, and a walking stick.

"What's the pop bottle for?" I asked.

"The bottle is for my beers."

"You have trouble walking?" Lesya asked.

"Well… I'm getting up there and I never take a bus or car… so it's getting tough on my knees."

We found a seat inside a nearby bar and immediately ordered a pitcher of beer.

"You want wings now?" asked Lesya

"No thanks. Not yet. Could we get Black Label? I'd prefer that."

"Shit shit shit!" he suddenly blurted out."

"What's wrong?"

"I've got one smoke left. Do you guys smoke?"

"Not me," I said, "but Lesya does."

"I'm out too. I'll go to the corner store and grab you some. Any favourite?"

"Export A. Mild. King size."

I didn't really know what to say or do next. Without a beer buzz, I wasn't much for small talk. I just never knew what to say to someone.

"So, Ryan, how long you been in this area?"

"About ten years, I guess."

"Why'd you pick this spot? Is it close to your place?"

"I've got a room in the Old Brewery Mission [a well-known Montreal shelter for homeless people]. It's a few miles from here. I don't start till 4:00 p.m., so I spend the day wandering around town, visiting art galleries, museums, libraries."

"I had no idea there was a schedule in Hoboland," I said.

"Guys can get pretty violent if you try and take their space. I've been beaten up a few times, even when I was in the right."

"So, why here?"

"Well, I know the area and just found that people here are more friendly. And there wasn't as much competition for space."

Lesya finally returned.

"Sorry, I didn't have enough cash on me. Had to find a bank machine. Here's your smokes."

"Hey… thanks a lot… fantastic, man." [Yes, readers, Ryan often ended his phrases with the word "man."]

"Are they the right type?"

"Uh… yes, they are. Thanks, man."

"So, Lesya, get this — Ryan is living at the Old Brewery Mission."

"We heard a rumour that you were living on the street. I guess that's not quite true?" she asked him.

"I did for about a year or so. I lived with a man quite happily about ten years ago, but then all these druggies kept coming in and stealing our stuff. I was doing sculptures and painting… and people were stealing it all the time for drug money. Then my boyfriend dumped me and I couldn't pay the rent. So I had to live on the streets."

"What about drawing?" asked Lesya, quickly changing the subject. "Do you still draw?"

"Yeah… sure… I keep this with me every day." He pulled out a coverless notepad. "Usually I'll sketch for someone if they ask. That way they're getting something for their money."

"This is beautiful," said Lesya as she leafed through the book.

"What do you draw?" I asked.

"Just what I see during the day. I get to people-watch a lot and I draw the interesting people I see. I try to imagine where they've come from, where they're going. What their lives are like."

"You seem pretty happy," said Lesya.

"Sure. I get up when I want. I see the city and meet lots of new people every day."

"I don't know about you guys, but I'm starving," said Lesya. "I'm gonna order something. You want some wings now, Ryan?"

"Okay. That sounds good. Maybe some more beer, too."

"We can do that."

"I gotta take a piss," said Ryan. "Be right back."

I was fascinated with Larkin. "It's like he just said 'fuck it' to life. Just decided he didn't want to be in the race and walked away. Lesya, this guy is something else."

"I told you!"

"But what can we do? I mean he seems pretty happy the way he is."

"Well… why don't we invite him to the festival? He doesn't have to be in the spotlight or anything. We could just invite him and he can hang out for the week. Maybe he'll get inspired."

"Oh, Lesya… I don't know. We don't know anything about the guy. He's not in great shape mentally or physically. What if he freaked out in the middle of a screening?"

"Ha… it might improve the screening!"

"True enough."

Unlike, say, Annecy festival audiences, who didn't hesitate to boo, whistle or applaud sarcastically, Ottawa audiences tended to be polite, maybe too much so.

"Look, Chris, it doesn't have to be a big deal. We can just invite him, give him a pass, maybe even a hotel room, and let him do what he wants. He obviously still wants to draw. And he can't really be happy trekking out here every goddamn day."

"Fine… okay… but let me talk, okay?"

"You're a beautiful person."

"Shut up."

Ryan finally returned.

"Your chicken wings are here. Eat up," said Lesya.

"Great man, thanks."

"I'll get more beer," I said. We were all starting to get a bit drunk now.

"So, Ryan," I started. "Lesya and I work at an animation film festival."

"Oh yeah… that sounds great, man."

"Anyway… we were thinking that maybe you could come to the festival this year. It wouldn't be a big deal. You wouldn't have to do anything. We'd just give you a pass and a free hotel room for the week. You can check out the different events…"

"What about beer, man. I need my beers."

"No problem. We've got a local beer sponsor. We'll keep your room stocked."

"Well… it sounds like a good idea. I might get inspired. Maybe people'll ask me for my autograph or somethin', man."

"That's possible. There'll even be studios there."

"Maybe they'll give you money to make a new film," added Lesya.

"Really?" Ryan's face lit up. "That would be grand, man. Grand."

"Well… anything's possible… but let's just keep it low-profile. It's just a chance for you to see what's up and hook up with some other animators if you want.

"Or hell," Lesya interrupted, "you can stay in the hotel room and drink beer all week, too."

"Ryan, I don't want to pry into your life," I asked suddenly, "but why'd you stop animating?"

"I never stopped, man. I just got tired of the industry. They're all a bunch of thieves. They stole my art. I got tired of giving it to them."

Ryan's voice was getting louder. His words were beginning to slur and his face was turning red.

"Those fuckers. FUCK THEM. They don't know anything about fucking art… bunch of soul suckers… taking everything you have and givin' you a fucking peanut for it. Then they make all the money off it. I ain't their monkey. Fucking assholes."

He worked himself into such a rage that the entire bar was now staring at us. He ranted on for a few more minutes before a waitress came over and asked Ryan to calm down. She was very sympathetic.

Seems it wasn't the first time this had happened here.

"You up for more beer, Ryan?" asked Lesya.

"Uh… yeah… yeah… sure. Sorry."

"Let's go somewhere else, okay?" I said. "I wouldn't mind having a few drinks."

"Umm… okay… sounds fine."

"I'll pay and meet you guys outside."

We headed for a bar across the street that Ryan often frequented. We didn't talk about animation or Ryan for the rest of the night. Just talked about music. Ryan said he was a drummer and still played in bands around town. We played pool. And then Lesya had us singing Ukrainian folk songs. I vaguely remember us driving Ryan back to the mission.

I thought a lot about Ryan. I even found copies of his films. I watched all four of them and was struck by how they seemed to foreshadow his life. His main characters were transients. They always seemed to be on the move. The films were beautifully drawn using watercolours, charcoal and even crayon to create rough, raw sketches of people on the streets, going about their business. There was a certain freedom in his films. His characters had no aim. They just roamed in and out of the frame. They were films about movement more than people. The freedom to move. Maybe it was a world he longed for. He spent most days sitting at a desk inside an old animation studio. The Film Board was a strange place. It was a weird union of artists and bureaucrats. It was a lively atmosphere no doubt, but there was something repressive about their studios. It was almost like being in a high school or a hospital. Everyone seemed cut off from one another. Granted, that was the nature of animation. Animators sometimes worked for years on a short film that very few, if any, people would see in the end. It was a crazy life. It required an obsessive and patient personality. You really needed to be a bit dysfunctional to live that kind of life. Maybe Ryan found it too repressive. Did he just decide to change his life and live like the characters in his films and be free of commitments and responsibilities?

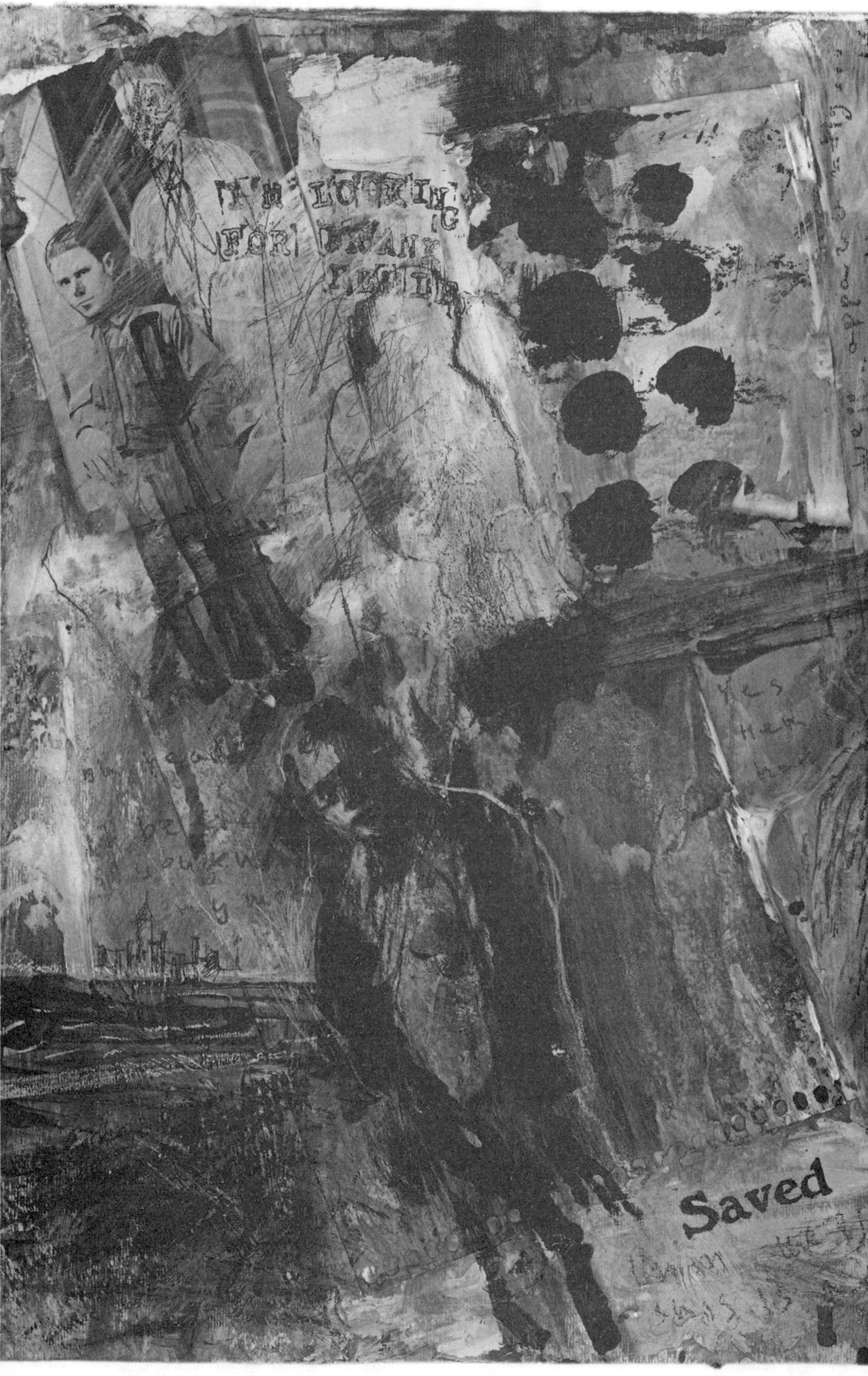
I'M LOOKING
Saved

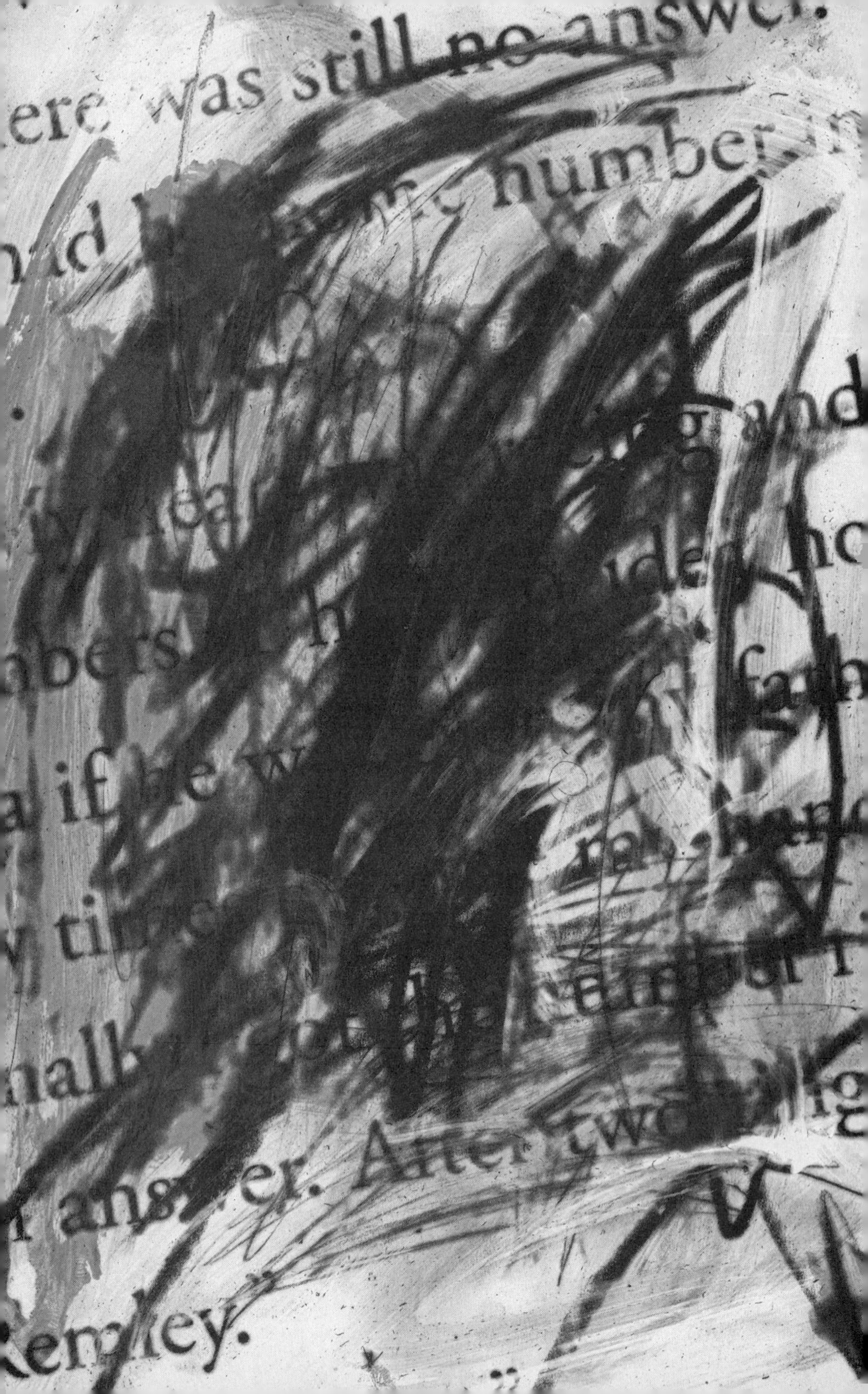
ere was still no answer.
number
and
bers
a if
answer. After two
Kempley.

After my first attempt to call Biopops at his family's cottage went unanswered, I tried a few more times.

There was still no answer.

I had his home number in Detroit and finally decided to call him there.

My heart was racing and my teeth were clattering as I dialed the numbers. I had no idea how this guy would react. Hell, I had no idea if he was even my father. I actually had to re-dial the number a few times because my hands were shaking and missing the numbers. Finally I got the number right and I took deep breaths as I waited for an answer. After two rings, a man answered. "I'm looking for Frank Remley."

"Speaking."

Umm… well… this is a bit of strange call. I have a bit of a bomb to drop on you. I don't really know how to say it… but umm… I think you're my father.

"Oh yeah?"

"I believe you knew my mother. You met her in Toronto and had, I gather, a one-night stand."

"Yes, I remember her. She had long blonde hair and glasses."

"Well… apparently… I'm the result of that night."

"It's possible."

His voice was warm and easygoing. We ended up speaking for a half hour. He told me that he had another son about four months younger with his first wife and a younger third son from his current marriage. Then he dropped a bomb:

"You know, I don't even know who my real father is."

"You're kidding."

"My mother had me with another man. They split up and she married another guy. They had four sons together, plus me."

"Wow. That's really amazing. It's bizarre. Did you ever find out who your real dad is?"

"Well… my mother doesn't like to talk about it… but I think it's this guy named Jimmy Leblanc. He's probably dead now."

"Jimmy Leblanc. Ha… he sounds like a Quebec gangster…. I don't really know what more to say. I'd obviously like to meet you, but for now maybe we can exchange some pictures."

"Sure. Sounds good."

We exchanged emails and addresses and said goodbye. I sat back in my chair, relieved but still shaking.

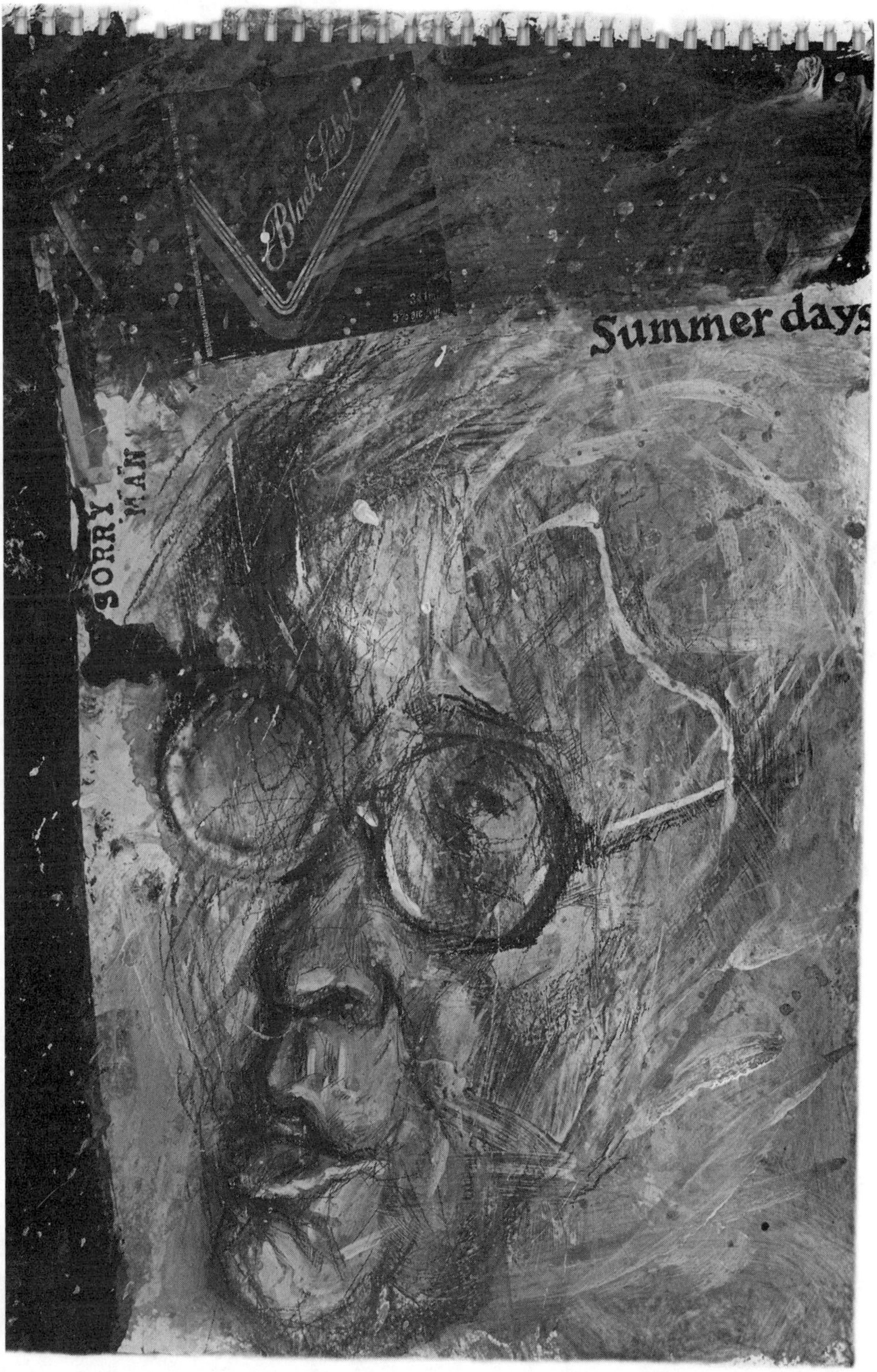
Black Label
Summer days
GORRY MAN

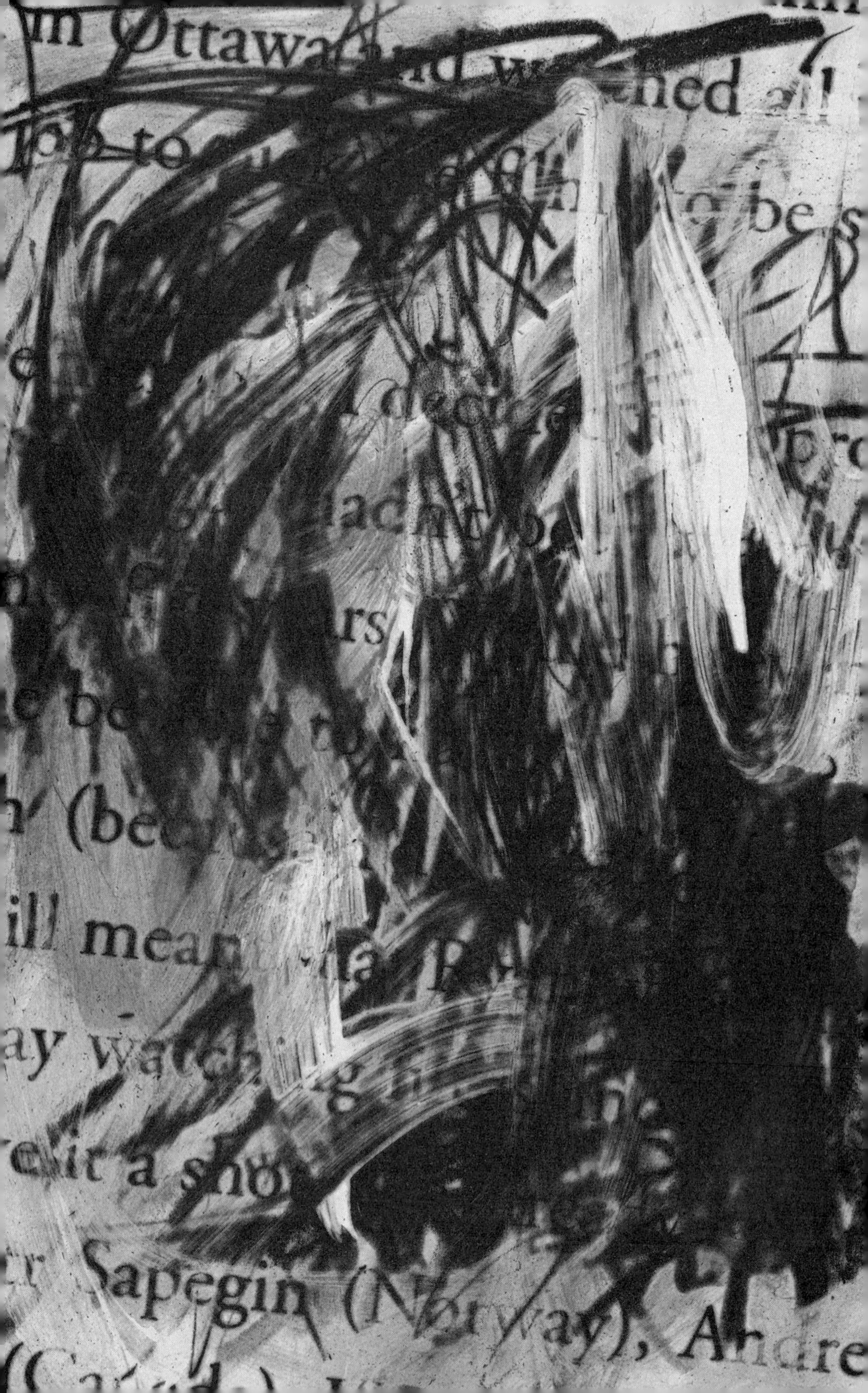
m Ottawa
ched
ill mean
ay watch
Sapegin (Norway), Andre

At the last minute, one of the festival's selection committee members dropped out. Each festival year, we brought in four or five people to serve as members of the committee. They usually spent just over a week in Ottawa and watched all the submissions we received. It was their job to pick the films to be shown in competition at the festival.

Down one member, I decided to approach Ryan about joining us. It was a risk. The guy hadn't been watching animation consistently for about twenty-five years. Would he even be able to judge the films? Hell, would he be able to hack the pace? The committee had fewer films to watch (because I'd taken over selecting the independent films), but it still meant that Ryan would have to be in a room about 9-10 hours a day watching films and discussing them. In the end, I figured we'd give it a shot. We already had three solid people on the committee: Pjotr Sapegin (Norway), Andrei Svisoltski (USA), and Chris Landreth (Canada). If Ryan turned out to be a problem, we'd still be okay.

Ryan agreed — once we assured him that not only would we come and pick him up, but we'd make sure that his expenses were covered (i.e., beer). Pjotr Sapegin was already in Montreal visiting his kids, so it worked out well. I drove there, picked Pjotr up and then stopped at the mission to get Ryan. I went in and asked for him at the reception. They called his room. No answer. I waited outside. Maybe 15-20 minutes passed before we saw Ryan turn a corner and approach the mission.

"Sorry, man, I had to get some smokes and beer. Hang on a second."

He then walked to the parking lot opposite the mission and disappeared around a corner. Another twenty minutes passed until he returned. This time, instead of the beer bottle, he had a plastic 7UP container. The mission doesn't permit booze on their premises, so Ryan keeps his suds in a secret spot in this parking lot. And naturally, using a plastic pop container enabled him to drink anywhere he wanted to.

His drinks sorted out, he now headed back to the mission. "I just gotta get my stuff."

About 10-15 minutes later, Ryan returned. I'd naively thought that he'd just be bringing some stuff for a few days, but in fact, he was bringing all of his belongings. It wasn't safe to keep them in the mission. So he came down with a duffle bag and a black plastic garbage bag. We dumped the stuff in the trunk and were finally headed to Ottawa.

While we were waiting for Ryan, I had tried to explain the circumstances to Pjotr. He was very easygoing about it all and almost immediately took on the role of big brother to Ryan.

After we dropped Pjotr off, I checked Ryan into his hotel. We decided to put him in the same hotel where we were doing the screenings. No point in taking any chances of losing him. After he dropped his stuff off, the first thing he wanted was a new supply of beer. We headed across the street to the liquor store. The beer was refrigerated in the back. I watched as Ryan took his time, carefully examining each brand of beer. Given my own heavy drinking at the time, I was quite impressed. He might be a drunk, but at least he was particular about what he drank. I just drank whatever. I drank to get drunk, not for the taste.

Ryan never did anything fast. His beer inspection went on for about five minutes before he selected some Belgian beers. It was only then that I realized he wasn't being particular about the brand of beer, he was, in fact, checking the alcohol content! The Belgian beers were 9-10% alcohol (compared to about 5% for standard beer). I laughed when I realized what was going on. Still, it was pretty smart shopping.

That evening, the committee hooked up and everyone introduced themselves. While they all recognized that Ryan was a bit different, no one really picked up on just who this guy had been until later in the week. The other committee members were all friendly and supportive of Ryan, but I still felt a bit uncomfortable. Would it look good that a respected animation festival was bringing in homeless people to be jury members? I used to joke with friends that I could round up a gaggle of hobos to do selection and no one would notice. It's such a difficult process in the end that you will never ever please everyone. I really believed (and still do) that an audience would hardly know the difference if we used hobos, housewives or whores.

Initially, Ryan didn't say much. He was always the last person to comment. That made it easier for him. He'd either go with the majority or, if everyone was undecided, he'd give an ambiguous response that suggested he wasn't sure either. I wonder what he was thinking. This was his first real exposure to animation since the 1970s. What the hell did he think of all this stuff that was being made? It wasn't just that computers dominated the process, but there was so much work being made for TV, commercials, music video, and even this new thing called the Internet. Ryan had worked in an environment where animation was made for artistic purposes. It was a cult art form done by a few. There was a bit of an industry, and some TV work being done, but nothing like the amount of work being produced in 2000. I imagine it must have been overwhelming. Did he think back to what might have been? Did he feel that he missed the boat? Maybe he was just thinking of the next beer. Who knows?

As the days passed, I could see Ryan's confidence growing. Andrei, Chris and Pjotr were really good to him. They were patient, and I remember that Chris, in particular, always tried to gently push Ryan to articulate his feelings about a work. I thought that was a nice gesture on his part. Other people might just say fuck it, let's move on. By the end of the week, Ryan was more confident in his opinions. Instead of giving monosyllabic feedback, he was digging deeper. This might have been the most honest period of my experiences with Ryan. His behaviour surprised me. He hardly drank that week (at least it wasn't visible) and he took the work seriously. I felt really good about what I'd done and it seemed that Ryan had a shot. That he did want to get his life back.

Emotionally speaking, the final evening was the most memorable. We had decided to have a screening of films made by the committee members. I consciously saved Ryan's work till the end because I thought that the other guys would finally realize just who this funny little man was. That's precisely what happened, and more.

We all have different memories of the moment after Ryan's films ended. I remember that there was complete silence until Pjotr or Chris said, "Oh my god, that was you?" Then, everyone slowly circled around Ryan and the questions about "what happened" began to flow. For maybe an hour, it was like being around a campfire. We were all mesmerized as Ryan told of his rise and fall as animator and artist. This was the moment that touched all of us. It was the moment I decided to write about Ryan and find out more of his story. It was the moment we wanted to figure out how we could get this guy back into animation. It was the moment that Chris Landreth got the idea to make a film about Ryan. It was a moment when we all thought we were going to save a man.

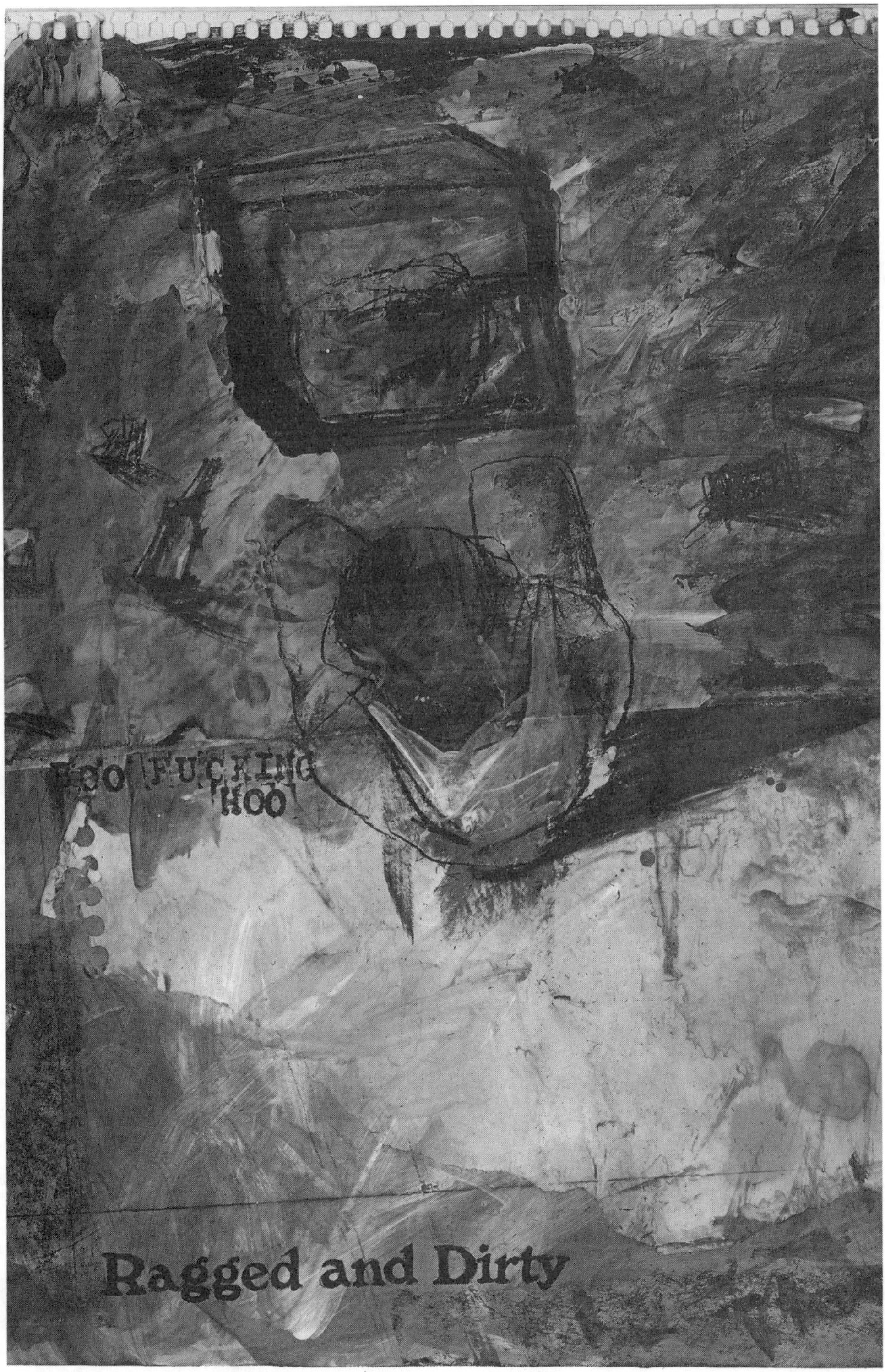
HOO FUCKING
HOO
Ragged and Dirty

But first a quick wank to calm

over a week. I would have fuc

woman, man or toilet roll.

it was better

embered po

ble. A

I wanted m

inherite

ial tha

were maga

ays seem

ngs be hidde

ress and go to sleep. Sleep

activity. My eyes wouldn

It was the night after the selection committee had finished. Everyone had gone, but I didn't want to leave. The festival gave me comfort, protection then; it gave me, me. Without it I was a shell. I had a home and a family, but I'd already been avoiding them for almost two years. I didn't want to go back because at our home I felt like a failure; it housed the real me, not the festival fraud.

I can't remember it very clearly, but I decided to stay in the hotel one more night. It turned into one of the weird nights of that time, a night when I think I wanted to die… or maybe it wasn't so dramatic. Maybe I just wanted to let go and become Ryan. It started like most nights. I hopped on the bed, turned on the TV, and started tossing back beers. I lost myself in the TV glow and let the booze buzz flush through my body. Only, there wasn't a buzz. After about five or six beers, I felt sober. No buzz. Maybe I was so tired I was just imagining that I wasn't drunk. Then again, these days it was taking a lot to get that happy feeling going. I felt a darkness growing inside me. Intense guilt and self-loathing. I stripped down to my underwear and got under the covers. I'll try and sleep. But first a quick wank to calm me down. I needed to get off. It'd been over a week. I would have fucked anyone who walked into that room, woman, man or toilet roll. Any hole will do. After I came, I remembered why it was better to be alone. I'd always felt uncomfortable. A big letdown, an exposure, a profound sense of humiliation. I wanted to flee from myself to escape some aura of shame that I'd inherited from somewhere. Maybe it came from all the porn material that Not Really My Pops kept hidden around the house. There were magazines, lubricant, dildos, blowup dolls, and videos. It always seemed like a secret, forbidden world. Why else would these things be hidden?

Finally, I fell into the mattress and tried to sleep. Sleep didn't come. My head was buzzing with activity. My eyes wouldn't shut. My frustration grew until I lost my temper and started thrashing my arms and legs against the bed. The bed didn't care. Finally, I flicked the TV. After a half hour, I was still glued to the glow. Fuck it. I got up, opened the hotel mini-bar and started downing the overpriced beers. I polished them off, but still nothing. I was getting angry now. Why on earth couldn't I get drunk OR at least pass out? I got up and started on the little liquor bottles. This oughta do the trick. Nothing but a slight tickle. That was it. There was no more booze. It was agonizing. I was not drunk. I couldn't sleep and there was no goddamn booze left to drink. It was 2:00 a.m. on a Monday. Too late to go out. Didn't want to go out. Darkness just fell over me. Never before had I felt in such a state. My mind and body felt like a hockey player trying to skate through a swamp in full gear. Slow, heavy, frustrating. Moving, but rarely making progress. Self-loathing slashed through me. Why though? Everything went okay. People were happy to meet Ryan. Ryan was having a good time and he clearly enjoyed the attention. Was it just that feeling of alienation? Everyone had gone and now I was just left alone. I was face-to-face with only me on this night. There was no escape from this room (in my mind).

Was this how Ryan felt? Is this what it felt like to give up on the world? Somehow I envied him. He just unplugged himself from the world. I didn't have that courage. I had few friends and continually changing staff at a job I faked my way into. And my wife? I was abusing her really. Not physically. I'd never laid a hand on her… but mentally. She had no idea who I was or who was gonna walk in the door each day. I lived in a world of extremes. I went from extreme anger to manic highs to absolute lethargy, as though the world could drop on me in a flash and I wouldn't give a damn. Being a husband, a father, a boss… they were crippling me. I'd made my bed, so to speak, but I couldn't sleep in it. These thoughts were racing in my mind. No coherence. Many voices. Another telling me to shut up and stop being so tragic. This one only made me more despondent. And then I'd feel bad for feeling so self-indulgent. People starve. Kids die. Who the fuck am I to moan about my oh-so-poor existence? Boo hoo. BOO FUCKING HOO. 'Course... then I'd just feel more wretched. This cycle of absurdity seemed to go on for hours. Sleep never did really come. The whole night I lay on the bed not quite awake or asleep.

Finally, the sun came. The TV was on. *Gunsmoke.*

I got up, packed my things, switched the TV off, and got the hell out of Dodge.

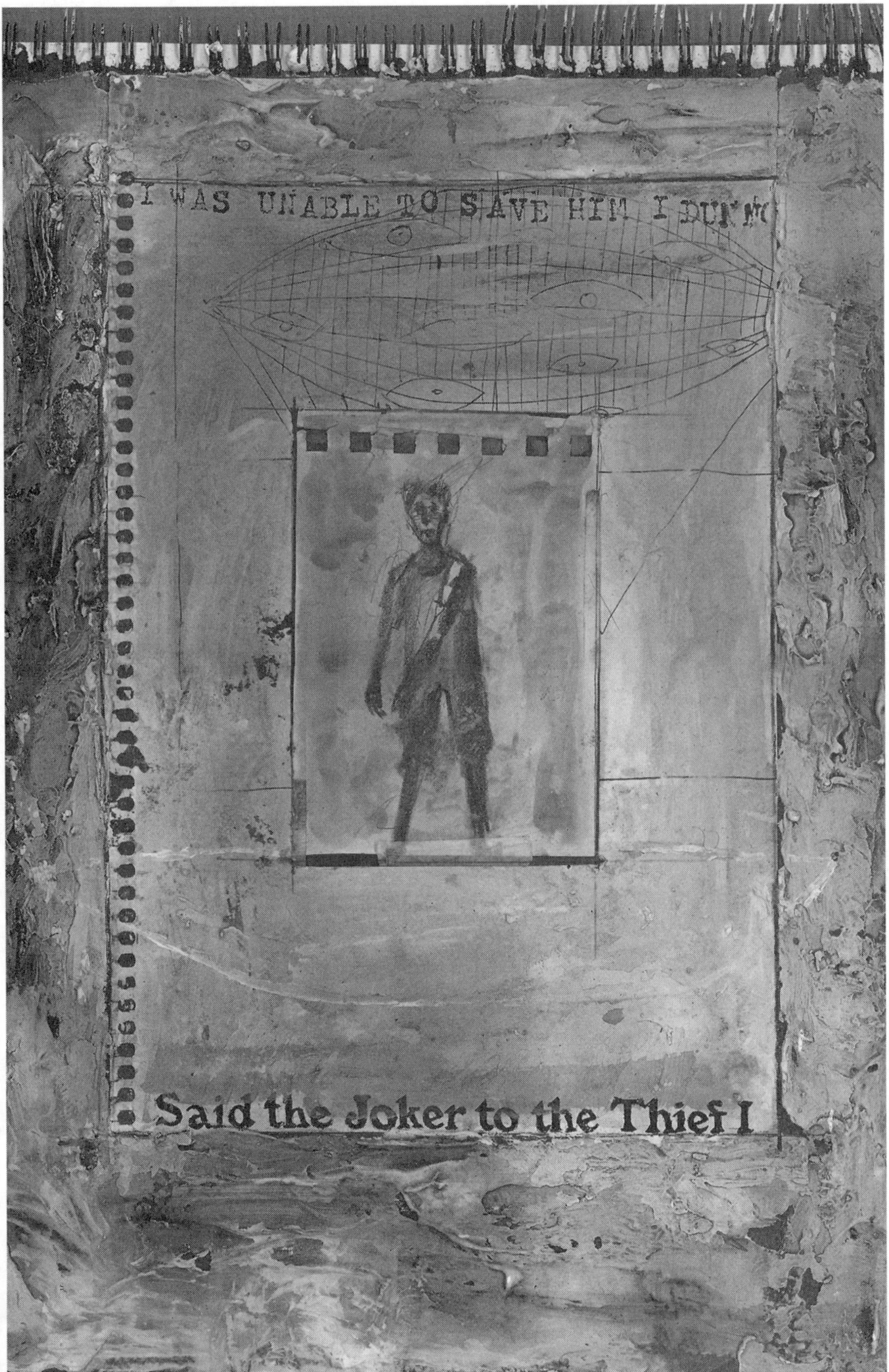
I WAS UNABLE TO SAVE HIM I DUN'M
Said the Joker to the Thief I

our

epy I told

h him He i

sor

ity

osed th

would

be

sion

ab

hi

ni

I co

d to

ant acro

w h

s born on

He was

ontreal

nald. Hi

an

plane

s a secretary.

Ryan stayed on in Ottawa for another week. I convinced a very hesitant Kelly to let him stay in our basement apartment. She thought he was creepy. I told her she was being paranoid. There was nothing wrong with him. He just needed some stability and encouragement. Still, I promised that he would not be left alone in the house. If I went out, Ryan had to go too. He was good about it though. He'd wake up around 10:00 a.m. and head out on his own. We wouldn't see him sometimes till 7:00 or 8:00 p.m. at night. He stayed for four-five days. On his last day, I asked him if I could interview him. All I'd ever read were vague rumours. I wanted to hear his story from him. He agreed and we headed to a restaurant across the street from the office. The beers flowed as we talked for a few hours. This was the story I pieced together:

Ryan Larkin was born on July 31, 1943. He was raised in Dorval, a suburb of Montreal. Larkin, a middle child, had two brothers: Roger and Ronald. His father was an airplane mechanic and his mom worked as a secretary.

Ryan remembers his parents as extremely hard-working people. "He was working as a jet engine builder at Dorval airport. We were living in Rosemount and then he bought a property in Dorval and built the house himself. He doing this and at the same time holding down a job. It took about 10 years to build. My mom was a secretary for the CEO of some company for many years. She was a very tiny person and very cute. A pixie type. Always collecting ornaments, stashing them on shelves. My parents were beautiful. They supported me."

As a child, Larkin loved to draw. "It was like I was given a natural talent to make images," he recalls. "I was doing portraits of my mom, dad and my brothers. They [drawings] were considered to be very advanced. I was called a gifted child. My father went out of his way to drive me out of Dorval all the way into Montreal to an art school for gifted children that was run by Arthur Lismer [a member of the so-called Group of Seven, which included some of Canada's most famous painters at the time]." By the age of about 10, he was already doing oil paintings.

As a teenager, Larkin began to do what most teens do: rebel and seek attention. "I was exhibiting the eccentric qualities of being an artist, which [my parents] objected to. Wearing my hair in different styles and doing unusual things. I was trying to perform and show off all the time. I was also trying to get attention. I was always a small, wee kid, right, and everybody else [his age] was famous for being in sports, for being handsome and strong and stuff. I was a great dancer. Rockabilly. Gene Vincent. There was a great record by Bo Diddley. I never went for the smooth Perry Como stuff. I was one of the original punk rockers."

One of his biggest heroes, though, was his older brother Ron. Ron drove around in a convertible and was very popular with the ladies. Larkin loved nothing more than to tag along in the backseat with his big brother. "I looked like a greaser punk and was the typical younger brother, always hanging out with him."

During the summer of 1958, 15-year-old Ryan Larkin, his brother and friends were playing on a boat in a lake. Something went dreadfully wrong. "There was a sandbar," remembers Larkin. "One of the girls was off taking a swim and she said, 'Oh, I'm having cramps.' My brother dived in and tried to bring her back but he had just gotten over some injury that he had about two months earlier and he started getting cramps. I dunno. He panicked. I couldn't operate the boat. It was a big cabin cruiser. And also, I couldn't swim so I couldn't save my brother. It was a very sad thing. It's been haunting me all my life. I should have done more. I tried to get into the water but I would have drowned as well. It made me so sad. I was unable to save him. It hit me very hard. I was on the boat and was physically unable to save his life. It was a major block for me. I felt terrible and missed him greatly."

Ron's death quietly fractured the Larkin family. Something changed. "I was always the goofy little guy, and they figured I goofed up again." Nothing was ever said, but he felt his family's scorching eyes. Larkin, a man who could bring beautiful images to life, could not save the life dearest to him.

Not long after, Larkin ran away from home. "I wanted some adventure and I quit high school. I ran away with a friend and we were on, like, a joyride heading west. We were obviously not supposed to be hitchhiking on the road at the beginning of the school term. A truck driver picked us up and we were sitting there, falling asleep. The driver made a stop at a truck stop and within a couple of minutes there was police."

The police picked the boys up and threw them in a cell. When asked for their names, they refused to speak. They were kept in jail for about a week, until Ryan slipped up and gave his name. "They interviewed us separately and we still refused to give our names. They finally tricked me by saying 'your friend Danny told us everything, so you might as well confess.' And I fell for it. Then they called my parents and my dad drove all the way out to Peterborough [about a five-hour drive from Dorval] to release us and drive us back home."

When Ryan returned home, his parents said, "What's wrong, Ryan? You have a nice home and everything is so beautiful."

Ryan told them, "'I can't stand high school. I can't stand going to school.' What I wanted was to go back to the Montreal Museum of Fine Arts school."

"My parents agreed to it," says Ryan, "provided that I covered the cost of tuition. So during the summer I had to get a job to put up the money for the tuition. I got jobs working in Lachine as an office boy, sorting mail, making $25/week. I did this every summer for three years. [Then] I dropped out of high school and started a three-year course at the Montreal Museum of Fine Arts school. I learned life drawing, sculpting, painting and design concepts."

Larkin excelled at the school and within a few years was being considered for a job at the National Film Board of Canada.

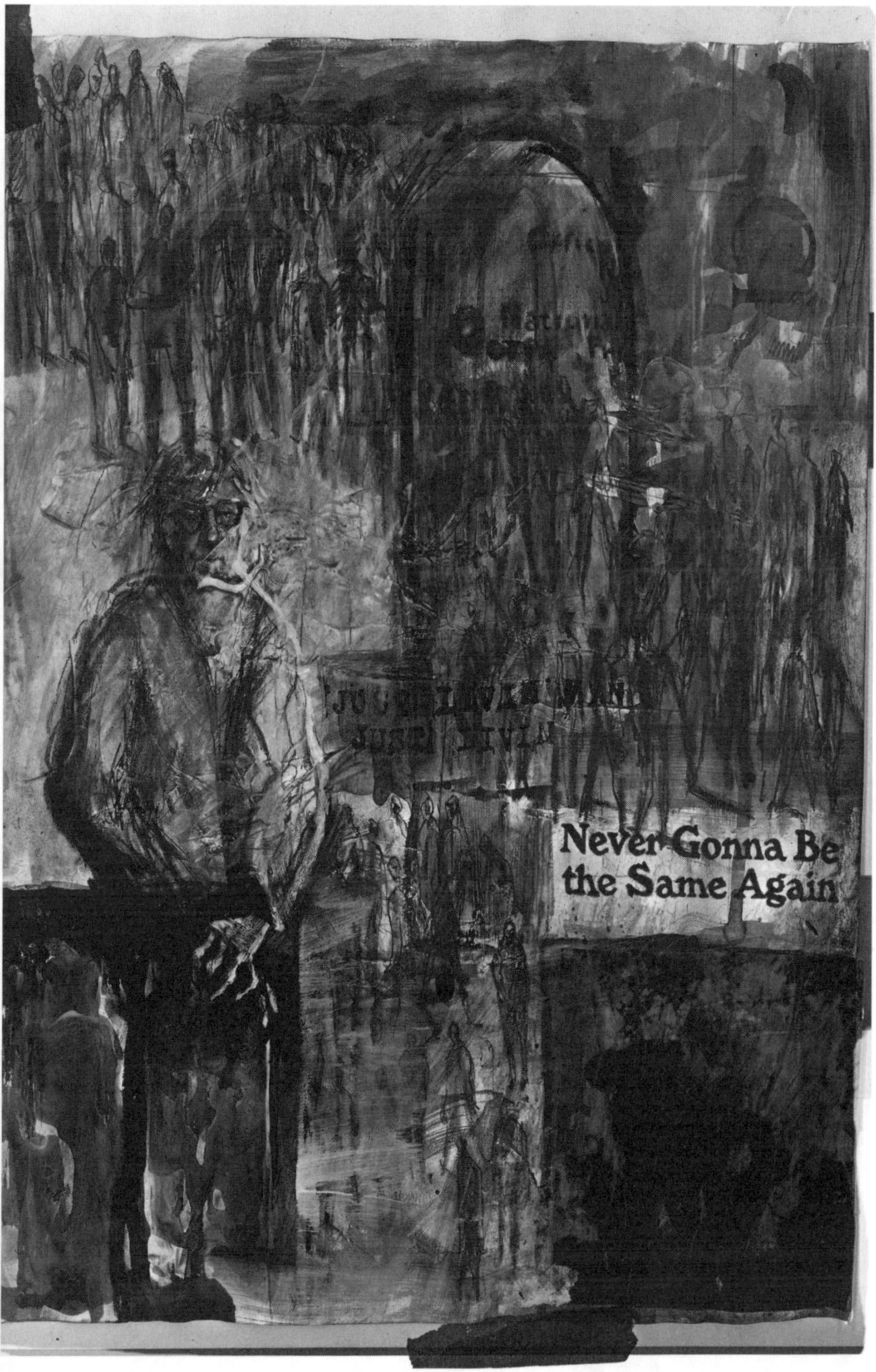
Never Gonna Be
the Same Again

nno, man. I should prob

Ryan, we've been plannin

You said yourself that yo

his is low-stress chanc

b... ng troubles

se... autor

...?"

much

, pro

s natural to be nervous,

ou think?

Ryan was scheduled to come back for the festival in September 2000, but a few days before the festival began I still hadn't heard from him. I called the mission, but he wasn't in. As usual, I left my number with instructions to call collect. A few days later he called. It turns out that Ryan was having stomach problems. I suspected that there was something more to it. He's a guy who likes his rhythm, and packing up to come to Ottawa again was undoubtedly a nuisance. He was also probably a bit scared. Even if we kept his appearance quiet, people would recognize him. It's not a big community and Ryan's name is fairly well known. Was he afraid of being turned into an icon or having to answer to his whereabouts the last twenty years? During our conversation I was a little pushy. I have to admit that I probably saw this as an opportunity to show everyone that I was a good lad, helping to resuscitate a dead man.

"Hello."

"Oh, hey, man… it's Ryan. What's happening?"

"Well… I was wondering if you're still coming to the festival."

"I dunno, man. I should probably stay here."

"But Ryan, we've been planning for this. This is a great opportunity for you. You said yourself that you wanted to get back into animating again. This is a low-stress chance to do that."

"I've been having troubles with my stomach lately. I'm gonna have to see a doctor."

"It's not serious, is it?"

"No, probably too much beer." He laughed.

"It's natural to be nervous, Ryan."

"You think?"

Suddenly I felt like I was talking to a little boy.

"Sure, this is a big step… but really, don't make a big deal about it. We're not even mentioning that you're here. You can just float around and check out the different events. If you get uncomfortable, you can just go back to the hotel room or, if it's really bad, you can go back to the mission. You're free to do what you want, but I really think you should at least give it a try. You've got nothing to lose."

"Okay… sure, man."

"Would you like someone to come and pick you up?"

"That'd be great, man."

"Okay… well how about 2:00 p.m. tomorrow? I can send a driver out there and he can take you directly to the hotel."

"Sounds great. Can you send some beers and smokes with him?"

"No problem."

"Black Label Ice and Player's Light. King size."

"Got it. See you tomorrow, then?"

"Okay."

"See ya tomorrow, Ryan."

"Uh… yeah… bye."

* * *

The two weeks leading up to the festival are madness. Imagine you were having a massive party at your house that's paid for by other people. That's sort of what organizing a festival feels like. They are your guests and you want to make sure everything is ready for them. The event itself only runs from Wednesday to Sunday, but with over 1000 out-of-town guests and about 60 events to coordinate, it's a year's work to get it ready. During the final weeks, we confirm hotel rooms, flights, details for all the parties and social gatherings. Will there be enough food and drinks?

There are media interviews, final programme book preparations, pass sales. Guests often arrive a day or two before the festival starts, so we've got to be ready even earlier. Often I have to drive out to get a guest because we haven't got a van rented yet.

The biggest test is the staff. Most of them have never experienced the event before, so they have no idea what to expect. Throughout the summer they've been working away in an office. The environment is casual, even a bit dull at times. It doesn't really prepare them for the ensuing madness that will eat up every waking minute of their lives for about a week.

Are the venues prepared? Is their staff adequately informed about the festival? Are the technicians and projectionists set up? It's only a matter of a spotlight and a microphone in most cases, but you'd be surprised how difficult a task that is, especially when you're dealing with rigid government union workers. Most of the time their staff are ill-prepared for the event. Most of the good venues in the city are government-run, and trying to deal with government workers is like trying to open a beer with your orbital bones: it's painful and leaves you wondering why you did it in the first place.

Once the festival has started, you can't do much more than just let it go on its merry way. The best way to handle things once it's underway is to, as the old philosopher Heraclitus said, "expect the unexpected." If you followed that advice, you'd be okay.

* * *

Ryan's presence went virtually unnoticed until the weekend of the festival. By this time, the bulk of the audience and guests had arrived. Until then, Ryan just went to screenings, hung out at our festival bar, and pretty much kept a low profile. However, on Friday night at the bar, a few people approached me and asked if that was really Ryan Larkin sitting over at the corner table. Naturally, a few of the older animators recognized Ryan — even in his sickly state. I said that it was him, but that we were trying to keep a low profile.

"Do you think it'd be okay if I went and spoke to him?" someone asked. “I haven’t seen him in years.”

“I’m sure he’d like that.” Soon, a few old-timers from the animation industry were sitting with Ryan, buying him drinks and talking about the apparent “good ol’ days.”

Ryan seemed to love the attention, particularly since everyone wanted to buy him a drink or bum him a smoke (he had packs in the hotel room, but he never missed a chance to take a smoke from someone).

“What have you been doing all these years?”

“Are you still drawing?”

“I heard you were dead.”

No one had the nerve to ask Ryan how he had got to this stage in his life. They asked what he was up to. “I’ve been doing research,” said Ryan, who certainly seemed able to laugh at himself. Some of the younger animators who’d joined in asked about his films (I guess they’d seen his films in their schools). “What was your inspiration?” and stuff like that. I could see that Ryan was really getting a buzz from the attention (and the booze).

The next day, word had spread throughout the festival about Ryan. During the last two days, people came up to him to chat. Every night, young and old animators were approaching his table with beers, a twisted offering to a fallen god. All Ryan had to do was sit there and answer questions. What did he think of today’s animation? How had the films changed from his time? Then the cautious, “So, Ryan, whatcha been up to?”

Ryan was good with those. He said the same stuff he had said to Lesya and me: “Just livin’, man, just livin’. I got tired of people stealing my art, or being exploited, so I turned my back on it.”

I found myself increasingly annoyed. I really wasn’t sure why. Was it Ryan’s scripted lines that gave me this feeling that he’d been doing this before? That what we were doing wasn’t so unique? Or was it the way people flocked to him?

Why is it that we wait until a person falls before we take an interest in them?

* * *

The festival ended. It wasn't a great year for films, so Ryan easily stole the spotlight. On the final night, all sorts of people approached Ryan about making a new film. He said he was eager to get started and that he had many new ideas. Numbers and addresses were exchanged.

Everyone left the festival feeling good.

Ryan was gonna be saved.

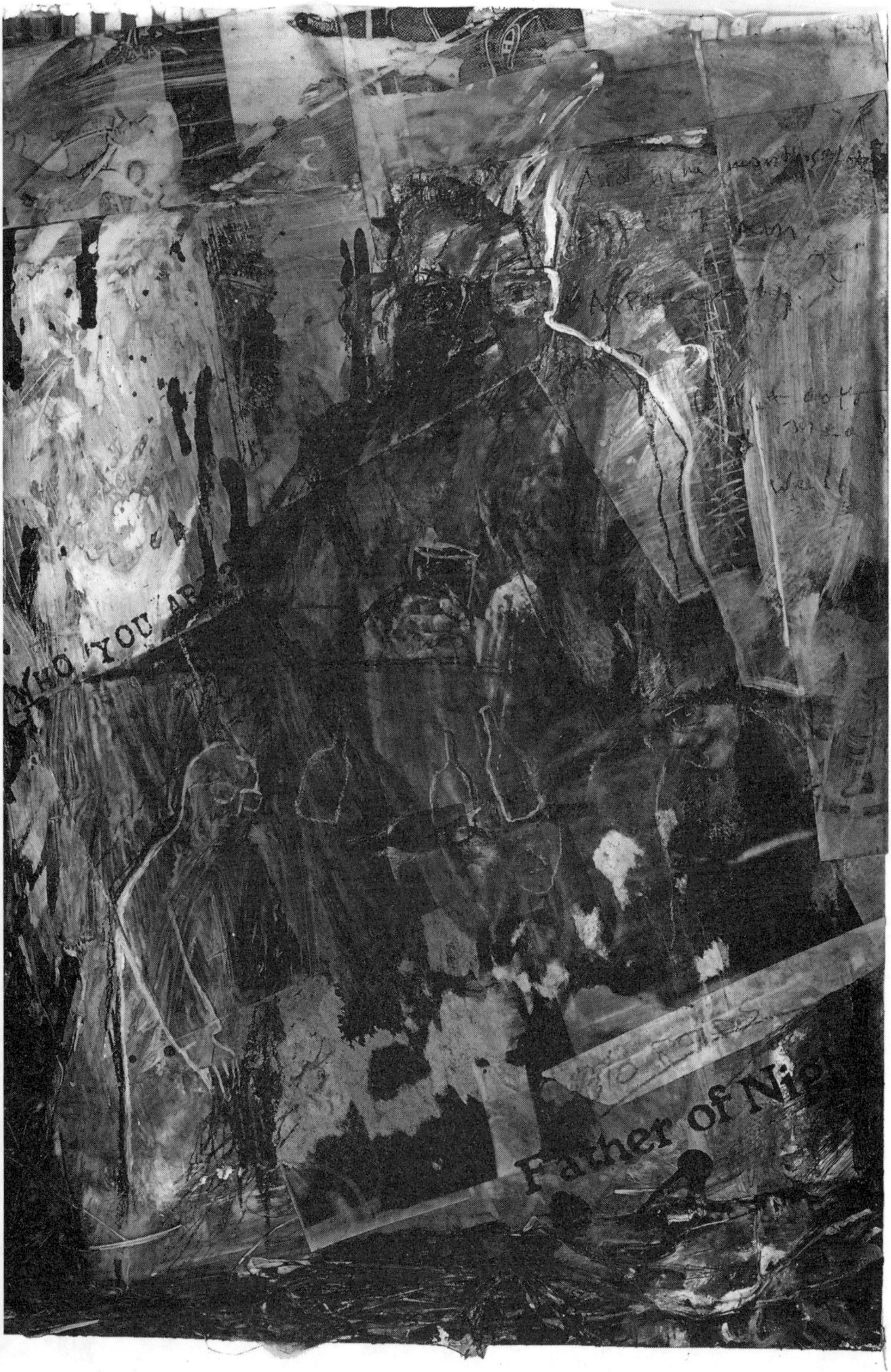
WHO YOU AR
Father of Ni

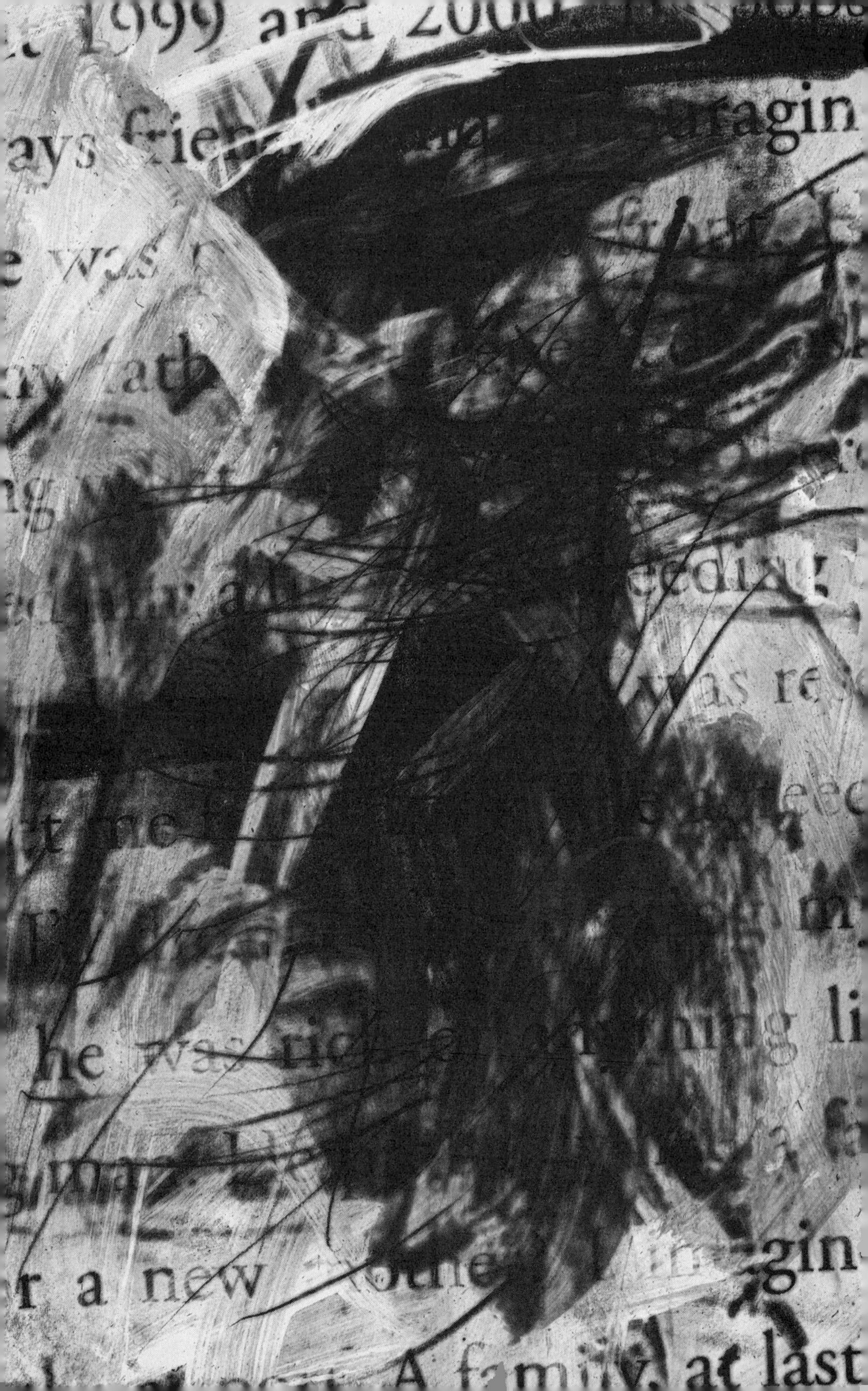
1999 and 2000
r a new
A family at last

Throughout 1999 and 2000, Biopops and I exchanged emails. They were always friendly and encouraging, but soon I got the sense that maybe he was putting on a front. He wouldn't actually admit that he was my father. He repeatedly asked if it really mattered. I kept suggesting we at least meet, but there was no firm response.

Finally, I fed him a line about needing to be in Detroit to interview an old hockey player for a book I was researching. I asked if he'd be willing to meet me for a drink. He agreed.

For years I'd dreamed of meeting my biological father. I didn't imagine that he was rich or anything like that, just that he was a happy, loving man. He probably had a family. Maybe I had brothers and sisters or a new mother? I imagined a great meeting. We all embraced at the airport. A family, at last.

Downtown Detroit was a like a big-city ghost town. Huge buildings stood alone, empty. There were hardly any people on the streets. It was a strange, disconcerting place. A sort of purgatory, a waiting room before you got to hell.

I stayed in a hotel in downtown Detroit. It was built in 1927 and was once one of Detroit's finest hotels. However, the hotel's glory had long since faded. The walls were cracked. Fixtures unrepaired. Carpets stained. Sheets stained. Shit in the toilet. And to top it off, some friendly rats were on hand to greet you at your door.

Biopops came to meet me in the lobby. We shook hands and quickly scanned one another. There was no obvious resemblance.

"Hi," I said. "Thanks for coming."

"No problem."

"Well, should we go somewhere? I don't know the area at all."

"Sure, there's a good old bar called Cobo Joe's near here. It's usually a hangout for Red Wings fans after the game."

As we walked, we talked about everything but our reason for meeting. He spoke about recently being laid off from his job and getting a new one with a mobile phone company. He was a salesman and not the successful businessman, rock star, writer I always imagined. I told him about the animation festival, my wife and son. Then we just talked hockey. Even though he was originally from Toronto, and he naturally rooted for the Red Wings, he had always been a Canadiens fan.

"That's funny because everyone in my family was a Leafs fan except me. I liked the Bruins as a youngster... mostly because an uncle bought me a Boston jersey, but when they kept losing to Montreal, I switched over to the Habs [nickname for the Canadiens, short for Habitants, the name for the original French settlers in Canada]. And even though we've finally got a team in Ottawa, deep down I'm still pulling for the Habs. There's just something about them. Maybe when the Senators prove that they can win, things will change."

We arrived at the bar. It was small and dark. The walls were covered with sports memorabilia. But this wasn't your typical faceless modern sports bar. This place creaked and cracked. It had been here since the 1930s.

"I'm sure [Ted] Lindsay and [Gordie] Howe hung out here in their day," said Biopops.

"Wow... yeah... this place is pretty amazing."

Dour drunks lined the bar. We grabbed a table near the old jukebox. George Jones was belting out "She Thinks I Still Care."

We ordered drinks and talked more and more hockey. He told me that he'd gone to the same college as Ted Lindsay's daughter and asked why I was interested in him.

"There's just something so unique about the guy. He was this maniac on the ice, yet off the ice he was one of smartest guys around. When he discovered the players were possibly being screwed out of retirement pay by the owners, he put his career on the line to make things better for the other players. He was willing to sacrifice everything to help and save others. Everyone talks about Howe and Richard [Maurice "Rocket" Richard, the great Canadiens player of the 1950s] and Gretzky being heroes, but to me, Ted Lindsay was the real hero."

"I remember when he was coaching the Wings in the 1970s," said Biopops. "I used to go to a lot of the games. They were a horrible team. It was frustrating for him. He was used to winning. He did everything he could to make them better, but he just couldn't do it. The media loved him though. He wasn't afraid to say what he really felt."

"That's what I admire about him," I said. "He had integrity and values. He never ran away from anything."

"So you're gonna write a book about him?"

"Well… I'm gonna try. I'm supposed to meet him tomorrow," I lied. "I've spoken to him a few times on the phone (which was true). He was really friendly and supportive of my proposal. But I'm not sure he's ready to tell his whole story. I can't tell if he's modest or if he's got something to hide that might damage his image."

"You ever read about Doug Harvey? He was involved with Lindsay and the Players' Association. That guy had quite a story."

"I've sort of heard about him. Didn't he end up living in a railway car or something? Was a drunk and lost all his money?"

"Something like that. He was a fantastic hockey player in his time, but he drank. So many of them drank."

"I don't understand how they could drink so much and still play effectively."

"Well, I guess it was their age. When you're in your twenties, you can get away with that stuff. But eventually it catches up with you. That's what happened to Harvey. By the end of his career he was a bloated whale. I heard he even played some games drunk."

"Is he still alive?" I asked.

"I think he died in the 1980s from, no surprise, cirrhosis of the liver or something. Someone should tell his story."

I was amazed at how easily we spoke. Even before we were into our third or fourth drink, hockey was providing a comfortable topic. It felt like we'd known each other for years. I was excited. This was my real father. There was no doubt now. We both liked hockey, the Habs, Lindsay, booze, AND we didn't know (at least till now) who our real fathers were.

I finally found the nerve to get to the topic.

"So, that's pretty amazing that you don't know who your real father is. That's quite a coincidence. What's that line from the Bible… 'sins of the father will be visited upon the son?'"

"Well, yeah, but does it really matter in the end? My stepfather was decent and I got along with my brothers. I was a relatively happy kid. I'm not sure how important it is to really know. What will it get me?"

I felt a sudden twinge in my stomach. "Well, certainty. Don't you want to know where you come from? Who you are?"

"What does that matter? What does it matter if I find out that Jimmy Leblanc is my real father? What does it mean? Sure, I'll know what my last name was, but will it tell me anything about who I am now? If I say I'm your father, what difference will it make? Will it change your life?"

"Of course it would. Be nice to know if there are any health issues on that side of the family. I've also got a son. He's gonna wanna know his roots too. Look… I'm not out for your money, I'm not out to force you into my life. I'm not expecting you to be instant pops. I just want to have some certainty about where I come from. I was clearly an accident and I could feel that. My mother blamed me. I was her albatross. A reminder of a night when her life went to hell (in her mind). She took all her hate for you out on me."

"So what happened that night?" I ask him. "Do you remember?"

"Vaguely… but I think she was at a bus stop in Yorkville in Toronto. She was being hassled by some guys. I pulled up in my car and asked her if she needed a lift. She got in. We ended up driving, I think, to her grandmother's apartment. We talked, had some drinks, and, well…"

"And nine months later… here I am."

"Apparently."

"What do you mean?"

"Well, your mother was dating another guy at the time. He had stood her up that weekend."

"So you're saying you might not have been the father?"

"Well, it could be."

"No. I've already broached this subject with her. I asked her point blank after I spoke with you for the first time. She hadn't even had sex with the other guy. You were her first."

He said nothing.

"Did you know that she came to your parents' house after she learned she was pregnant?"

"Yes. I was in Detroit at school then. My mom called me after. They wanted me to stay in the U.S. They were afraid that I'd be arrested if I came back to Canada."

"Really? That seems a bit much. I heard that your mother was quite cruel to my mom. She told her that she didn't believe her and that her son certainly wasn't the father. That was a pretty nasty thing to do to a teenager. Especially from a woman who seems to have done the same damn thing."

"Well, you have to understand that I'd only met your mother once. She spent a lot of time complaining about her boyfriend. She was really pissed off at being stood up. It seemed a bit strange that after having sex just once that suddenly I'd be the father. She'd been with this guy. Surely, they'd slept together before."

"Well, according to her, they didn't. You were the first. Look… I'm not stupid enough to believe that we can become instant father and son, but I just need some certainty, some closure."

"Do you really think this is going to change your life? That everything will suddenly be alright?"

"I don't know."

Silence followed. I took a swig from my beer. It must have been my sixth or seventh. He was into rum and cokes now. I wondered how he was gonna drive all the way out to Oakland county.

"I gotta hit the toilet."

I was left alone. I was delirious and demoralized. I was sure he was my father. He remembered everything about the night with my mother. Everything fit, so why wouldn't he admit that he was my father? What was he afraid of? I made it clear that I didn't want anything other than an answer.

He finally returned to the table.

"So, do you have a family?"

"Yeah, I've got a wife and a teenage son. I've also got another son from my first marriage. He's about your age, just a few months younger."

"Shit, you really got around, didn't you?"

"It was the sixties. That's what we did back then," he said to explain his drunken one-night stand with my mother.

His response made me angry. In one heartless phrase he brushed off my birth. "It was the sixties." As though that was the secret phrase that excluded you from taking responsibility for anything. It was the sixties. We fucked everyone, got stoned and rebelled, man. Did they think that it was a time capsule, that once the decade was over they could just move on and forget that the "summer of love" never happened? Because he and my mom got drunk and silly one fine night that he gets a far-out groovy free pass simply because it was the sixties, man? It was bullshit anyway. He took responsibility for the kid he had four months later. Why him, but not me?

That's what I wanted to say to him. But I said nothing. I was too scared to piss him off. Instead, I sipped my beer and nodded my head like an obedient little child. I did at least get up the nerve to ask him if we could simply go and verify this once and for all.

"Would you at least be willing to do a paternity test so that we could resolve this? I've no idea how these things work or where to go, but I'm sure we could find someplace."

"Sure," he said.

We finished our drinks and got up to go. We were both quite drunk by now. At least, I was. I was an emotional mess inside.

"Well, I'm here for two more days. Maybe we can get together again? Maybe we can find a place to do a test? Would you be open to that?"

"Sure, why not?"

"Should I call you?"

"I'll call you."

He never called.

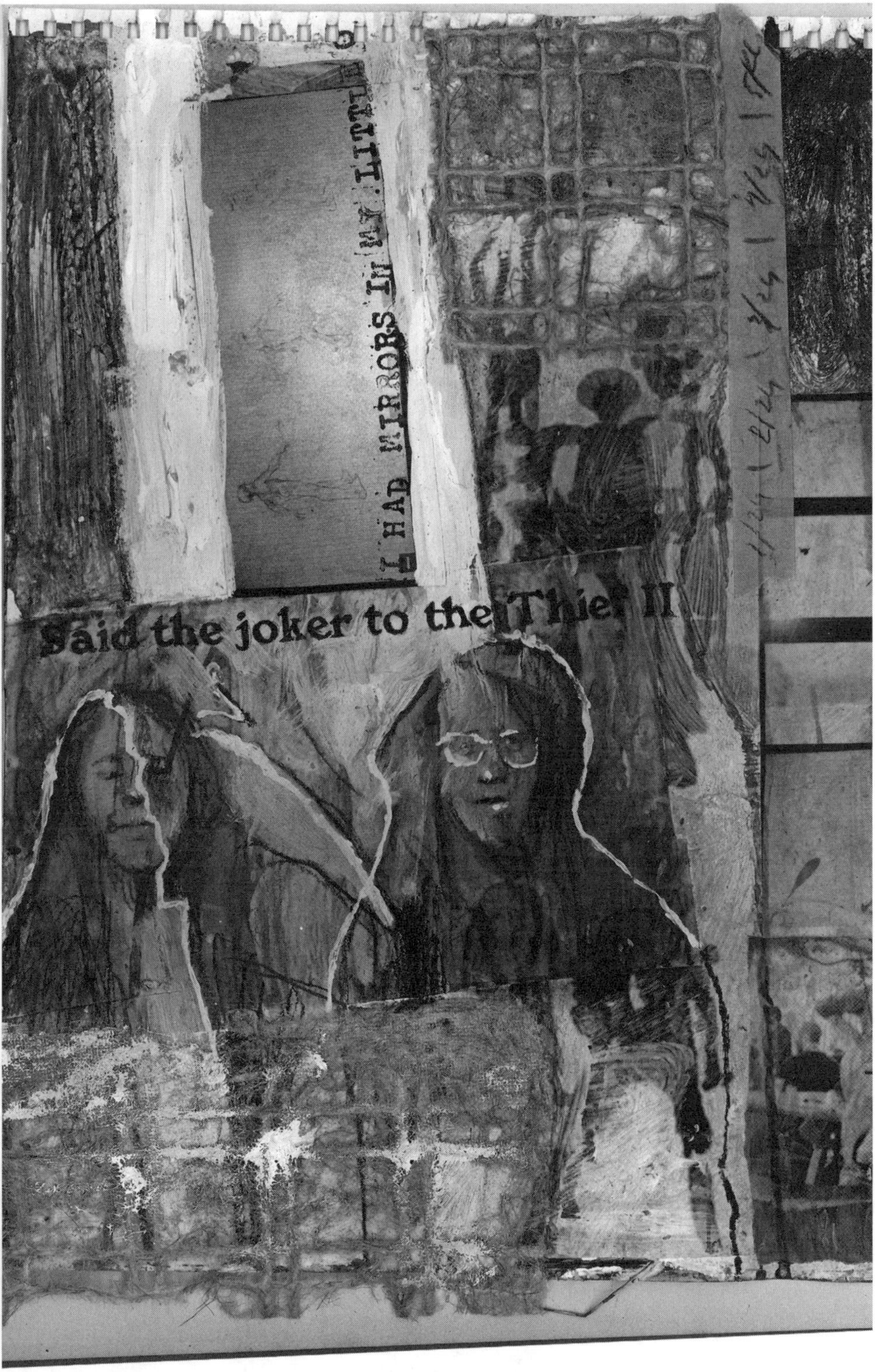
I HAD MIRRORS IN MY LITTL
Said the joker to the Thief II

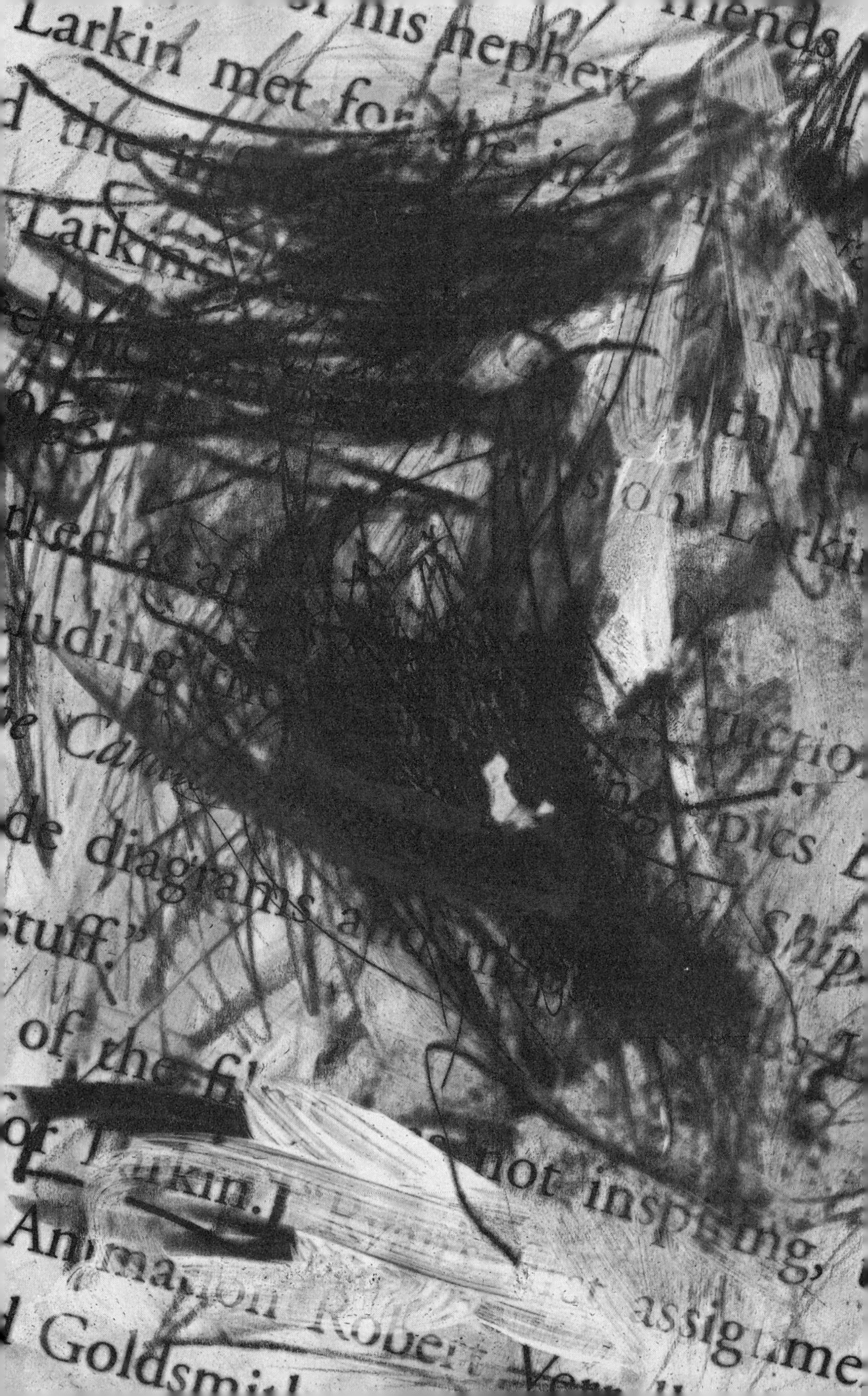
his nephew
friends
Larkin met for
Larkin
son. Larkin
luding
de diagrams
pics
stuff.”
of the fi
kin.]
not inspiring,
assignme
d Goldsmit

While working in Lachine, Quebec for "the Hudson Bay power dam thing," Larkin's uncle, who was friends with an NFB animator, arranged an interview for his nephew.

The man Larkin met for the interview was Sidney Goldsmith (who designed the influential Oscar-nominated short, *Universe*). Impressed with Larkin's portfolio, Goldsmith hired the young artist to work in the technical animation division. Larkin was hired by the NFB on July 2, 1963.

He initially worked as an animator on instructional films for the army and navy, including the spine-tingling epics *Ball Resolver in Antic* (1964) and *The Canadian Forces Hydrofoil Ship: Concept and Design* (1967). "I made diagrams and maps," recalls Larkin. "Very cut-and-dried, boring stuff."

While the content of the films was not inspiring, the overall experience was pivotal for Larkin. "Ryan's first assignments," says former Head of English Animation Robert Verrall, "involved the talents of René Jodoin, Sid Goldsmith, Kaj Pindal, Ron Tunis and others — not bad company for a 19-year-old apprentice. Such programmes were part of the NFB mandate, and allowed the hiring and training of people who would otherwise not have seen the inside of the place."

During the mid-sixties, Larkin became friends with Norman McLaren, Guy Glover and Grant Munro. The relationship with McLaren opened Larkin up to a completely new world. "They were sophisticated. They had huge libraries and invited me home and showed me their libraries. It was fascinating. I was just working-class. In my house we had pictures of airplanes." Larkin absorbed books, paintings and classical music. "I was young and really impressed with all this new information."

At the urging of Wolf Koenig, McLaren had recently begun holding an after-hours session in a small room at the Board. During these sessions, McLaren set up projects for the eager young artists (including Pierre Hébert, Co Hoedeman and Ralph Abrams). "He'd give us 16mm cameras and teach us the fine aspects like calibration and how to use our senses. He had a test that involved taking a cut-out of a round ball and shooting it single- and double-frame." Artists were given a roll of film to shoot whatever they wanted. Animation came as naturally to Larkin as drawing. "Norman said I had natural control over timing and pacing over any given object."

Larkin developed a unique technique involving stop-frame action with charcoal that was easy to erase. Using a strong sheet of paper, Larkin was able to draw deeply into the paper and still erase it. McLaren was so impressed that Larkin was given a budget to release one of his after-hours experiments as a film.

Utilizing this new technique, Larkin made a one-minute test film called *Cityscape* (1966). Inspired by an early Bob Dylan song, "Talkin' New York," this dark, nightmarish view of the city is filled with a mélange of strange characters coming and going. It is hesitant and sloppy at times, but also a shocking, raw and almost paranoid portrait of the cement garden.

Larkin shot *Cityscape* single frame and "the whole thing went whizzing by in 30 seconds. I didn't quite know what I was doing." Larkin extended the film by means of an optical imager, reprinting the frames and cross-dissolving them to give the film a natural-looking motion.

People at the Board noticed *Cityscape* and were taken by its originality. McLaren approached Board producers and asked that Larkin be given carte blanche to make any film using the charcoal technique. "They said, 'Here's a budget. You've got three months to make any film.' I spent a week wondering what I was going to do. One of Norman's friends presented me with a solo flute piece called 'Syrinx' by Claude Debussy. A French flutist recorded it and that was my starting point." Using the flute piece, Larkin then turned to the Greek story about Pan. In this tale of stalking, Pan is constantly hasslin' the hotty Syrinx for a little love. Tired of his come-ons, Syrinx asks Gaea for help. Gaea then turns Syrinx into a clump of reeds. Pan then takes the reeds and turns them into an instrument.

Larkin faced a number of problems before completing the film. The music was a key ingredient and had to be carefully timed and paced, but Larkin lacked the necessary money to buy the music. Instead, he found a member of the Montreal Symphony Orchestra to record it for less money. The music setback was minor compared with the realization that he had to reshoot the entire film: "First time I got off track and the images weren't coming off as beautiful as I wanted. I was getting nervous, but Wolf [Koenig] and Bob [Verrall] said, 'Go back and re-shoot the whole thing.'" Ah, the fortune of a court artist! Larkin reshot the film, this time concentrating more on the images and the body of Syrinx. The final product received excellent reviews and *Syrinx* (1965) won awards all over the world, including the Grand Prize at a children's festival in Iran.

Larkin was now living a princely life in downtown Montreal, continuing to paint and sculpt and surrounded by many friends. "I was always good at sculpting and doing three-dimensional sculptures. I began to see animation as a form of sculpting." He had a few small exhibitions and many people at the NFB purchased his drawings and paintings. Larkin gleaned his inspiration in cafés and bars, watching and absorbing the way people walked and talked and moved. He loved to watch people and would make sketches of people walking or get friends to pose. Larkin's friends were also doing more than posing, doing what kids were supposedly supposed to do: drugs. Ironically, Larkin wasn't into drugs at the time and instead played Virgil to his LSD-saturated mates. "They would experiment and I wouldn't. I made sure they didn't fly out windows."

After *Syrinx*, the producers told Larkin that he had to go back to applying his talents to public service films. He made, and remains proud of, a variety of educational films for St. John's Ambulance, an elaborate colour pastel clip on preventing forest fires, and a contribution to the NFB's exhibition at the Montreal Expo. "The Board had its own pavilion, called "Labyrinth," and they had multi-screens. I was asked by Roman Kroiter and Colin Low to put in a labyrinth, the old Greek idea, using the same style as *Syrinx*."

Following the Expo exhibit, Larkin put in a proposal to do a film based on sketches he had drawn of people walking around. The proposal was accepted and Larkin was given a year to do the project. However, because he dreaded the thought of repeating himself, the film took two years as Larkin worked to perfect new techniques. "I was developing my Oriental brushwork with water colours, and the human figures and the way that anatomy works, expressions of human behaviour, how funny they look sometimes when they're trying to impress each other with certain movements. I wasn't doing any rotoscoping, I was doing a lot of self-study. I had mirrors in my little office, and I would go through certain motions with my own body and was just going with pencil, ink and paper." In concentrating on motion and the details of the figures, Larkin abandoned background movement, instead choosing a blank white screen.

The result of this two-year project was *Walking* (1968), one of the most celebrated films made at the NFB and one that remains a major influence on animators to this day. Using a combination of line drawing and colour wash, Larkin observes the movements of a variety of urban characters. He weaves colours and sounds with an extraordinarily detailed visualization of faces, bodies, gestures and postures. A vivid imagining of the city and those within it.

Walking received an Oscar® nomination and Larkin travelled to Hollywood with his girlfriend, Felicity. The Oscars® provided Larkin with a chance to put his beatnik persona and wild wardrobe into practice. Larkin had hair that was about three feet long and made his own clothes. "I would sew together my own pair of pants in special colours. It was coming out earlier I think, I was always performing, trying to look outrageous by whatever standards were established, just being a punk." For the Oscars®, Larkin selected a flashy silk, wide-sleeved shirt and tight-fitting pants with bright colours.

Death once again stepped in Larkin's path. Walt Disney, who had ceased to breathe a year before, won the Oscar® for Ward Kimball's *It's Tough To Be a Bird.*

Around this time, Larkin also pitched a new project to the NFB. Little is known about the proposed film outside of what is contained in Larkin's files at the NFB archives. The proposal for *People Painting* is dated April 1, 1968. Larkin writes, "I've been interested in body painting (in particular face painting). I could take a child, for example, and draw lines over his face and end up with a caricature of what he might look like when he matures." The project, which would be made using pixilation, was recommended for programming as experimental and was to be part of a package called "Prayers" that Arthur Lipsett was putting together. There is no mention of why the film was never made.

Following *Walking*, Larkin once again returned to NFB public service films before being loaned out to a Vancouver art school. For eight months, Larkin ran an animation workshop. Each student worked in their own studio and Larkin would travel around visiting them, hanging out and directing them. Larkin encouraged the students to find their own voice no matter how wild their experiments turned out. Among these young voices, Larkin met a group of street musicians. "I decided that they would make a great focal point for my abstract images. There was a whole little gang of them with their own children and stuff, hippies I guess, really good musicians." Larkin's encounter led to his next film, *Street Musique* (1972).

Very much a film in search of itself, *Street Musique* opens with live-action footage of two street musicians before changing into a staggeringly animated stream-of-consciousness piece. A variety of creatures and figures float through the screen and undergo a continual metamorphosis. *Street Musique* is loosely divided into about five or six segments, all determined by the pace of the music. One of the most dazzling scenes comes in the second segment with a series of extraordinary impressionist landscape paintings. As with most of Larkin's work, though, you can feel the hesitancy. The film ends rather awkwardly, with the last image stopping to wait for the music. "What happened was, I ran out of ideas and I didn't know how to end the film, so I just ended it on a strange little character, wiggling away in his little dance, in a way suggesting that, 'This is to be continued.'" Structural critiques aside, *Street Musique* is a toe-tappin', knee-slappin', barn burner of a film, solidifying Larkin's talent as an artist and animator.

Street Musique did the festival circuit and won a Grand Prize at an Australian film festival. Larkin is particularly fond of this award because it was a live-action festival. "It was a ten-minute film up against all kinds of complicated feature films." Larkin received $3000 with the prize and, because he had a regular salary, he often supported other young artists with his prize money. "I had a nine-room flat in Montreal that I was renting for $100 a month, if you can believe it, and I'd give money to certain young people to experiment with their art and their music. I'd give them free room and board to hang around. In a sense, I had my own school." Larkin's generosity with people would come back to haunt him.

By this time Larkin was starting to get attention in the press. In a 1969 *Montreal Gazette* article, author Mark Slade deems Larkin "the Frank Zappa or George Harrison of animation films. He is at home in a world of movement, change, transition. Like millions around the world living in an electric space, his life experience is as much an art form, uniquely personal in style, as his work."

Slade saw Larkin as a sort of saviour of the NFB. In his opening sentence, he blasts NFB founder John Grierson for once saying that "the Board could only afford one world-famed animation artist – Norman McLaren."

For Slade, it was essential that if the NFB was to survive and to remain relevant it needed "people to organize experience, invent meanings for affluence, make sense out of information. [Otherwise], many young people of the sixties must live on the brink of a continuing crisis." Larkin, Slade seemed to suggest, was just the man to save the NFB from becoming a staid propaganda machine.

"Not only intensely aware of living in the twentieth century," says Slade, "[Larkin] has a talent for expressing the shifting gradients of his times. He is attempting to reduce the chaotic, the random, the complex to simple patterns — to a kind of joy, sometimes a fear or foreboding, that underlies everyday existence."

Larkin had no idea these things were being written about him, but he was aware that he was becoming famous. While he always liked attention, the pressures and expectations of fame quickly began to eat him up, turning him into an arrogant and increasingly paranoid person:

I had a problem with my ego. I sort of lost control for a while. I became too much of an icon. I became… (long pause)… too much self-centred. I wanted it to be simple. I couldn't go back 'cause I was too much in the spotlight. I couldn't handle fame. I wasn't properly educated. I couldn't control myself. I was prancing in front of cameras all the time. I began to despise myself. I did some good things, but I wasn't really a great filmmaker. I made some good films, but I was never really a good filmmaker. I went berserk. I was prancing in front of cameras instead of doing my work. I was just disappointed in my performance because it seemed to me that I was just performing in order to get my face and my image in front of my contemporaries and I was failing to do my real job which was to be a creative artist. I became an egomaniac, which I tried to put aside, but I was unsuccessful.

By 1972, Larkin's biggest problem was that he wasn't sure he had anything left to say. He had run out of ideas. In a desperate attempt to find something, anything, to say, he turned to drugs to try to reignite his creativity. It didn't work.

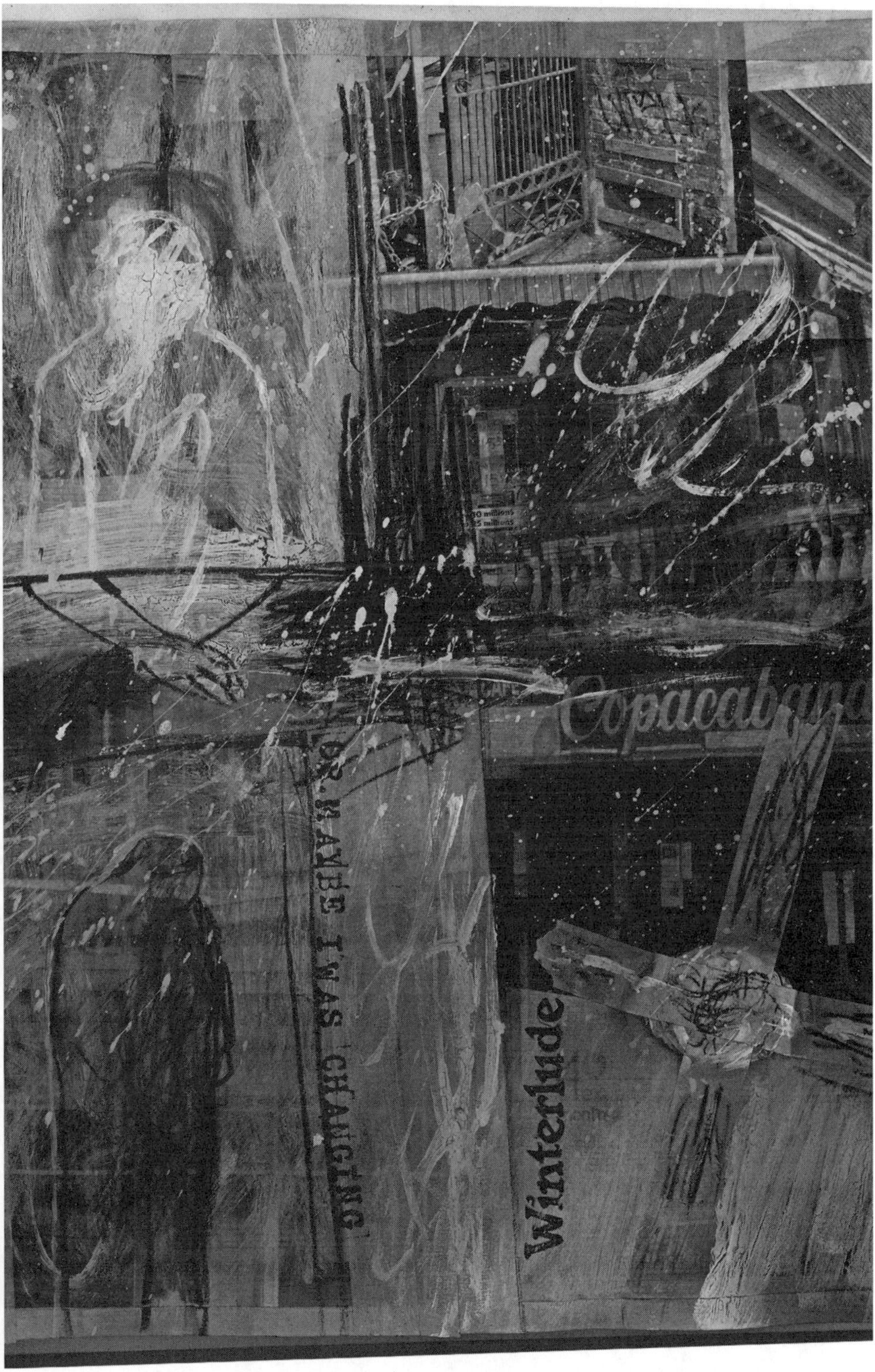
Copacabana
OR MAYBE I WAS CHANGING
Winterlude

colleagues
the evening
sure
the

After the festival I made a couple of tentative arrangements for Ryan to start making films again. He had the option of working here in Ottawa on a film with the local film cooperative or heading to Calgary where a group of animators had arranged for him to receive an artist-in-residence grant for a year. Ryan didn't seem interested. He didn't want to leave town for fear his welfare cheques would be taken away from him. When I suggested the Ottawa option, he said, "Sounds great, man." But he really didn't seem interested, so I backed off.

* * *

The winter came and life moved on. My drinking had reached dangerous territory. I had just come back from an animation festival in Seoul, Korea, where I behaved like an ass. I drank *all* the time: on the bus, off the bus, even during presentations, where a stack of beer cans littered the table I sat behind. One night a couple of us helped hijack the festival director's chauffeur-driven car. We had him drive to the red light district in Seoul. The director wasn't impressed. In the end, neither was I. During the final night of the festival, I observed a drunken colleague acting like a complete ass. He was ridiculing many of our other colleagues. I'm not sure why it bothered me so much, but it did. As the evening worsened, I developed a conscience and began questioning the things I was doing.

* * *

I saw Ryan once that winter. Kelly and Jarvis were with me. We sat down with him and had a bite to eat. As we spoke, he said a lot of the same stuff that he'd said to Lesya months earlier. I felt anger surging within me. I was starting to hate Ryan. I had this feeling that maybe he was just toying with us all. That he was putting on a performance for people in exchange for his necessities: beer, food and smokes.

I think Ryan was also afraid. For all his talk, I didn't believe he felt he could draw anymore. He mentioned that he ran out of ideas after *Street Musique*, so perhaps that's another reason he ran away from animation. He simply had nothing left to say. You can certainly see a flicker of that emptiness in his films. They're all rather feckless and undetermined.

Or, maybe I was changing.

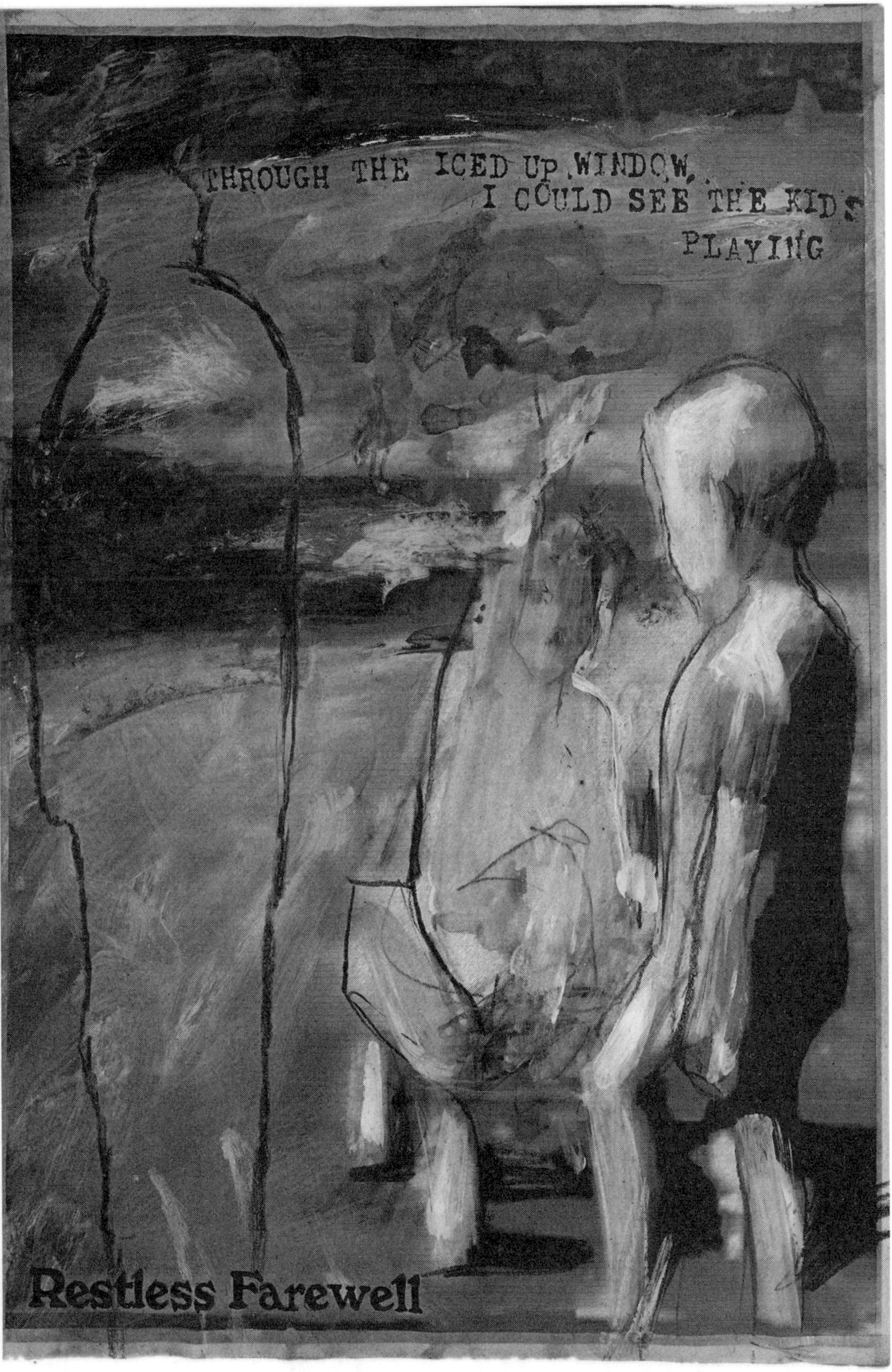
THROUGH THE ICED UP WINDOW,
I COULD SEE THE KIDS
PLAYING
Restless Farewell

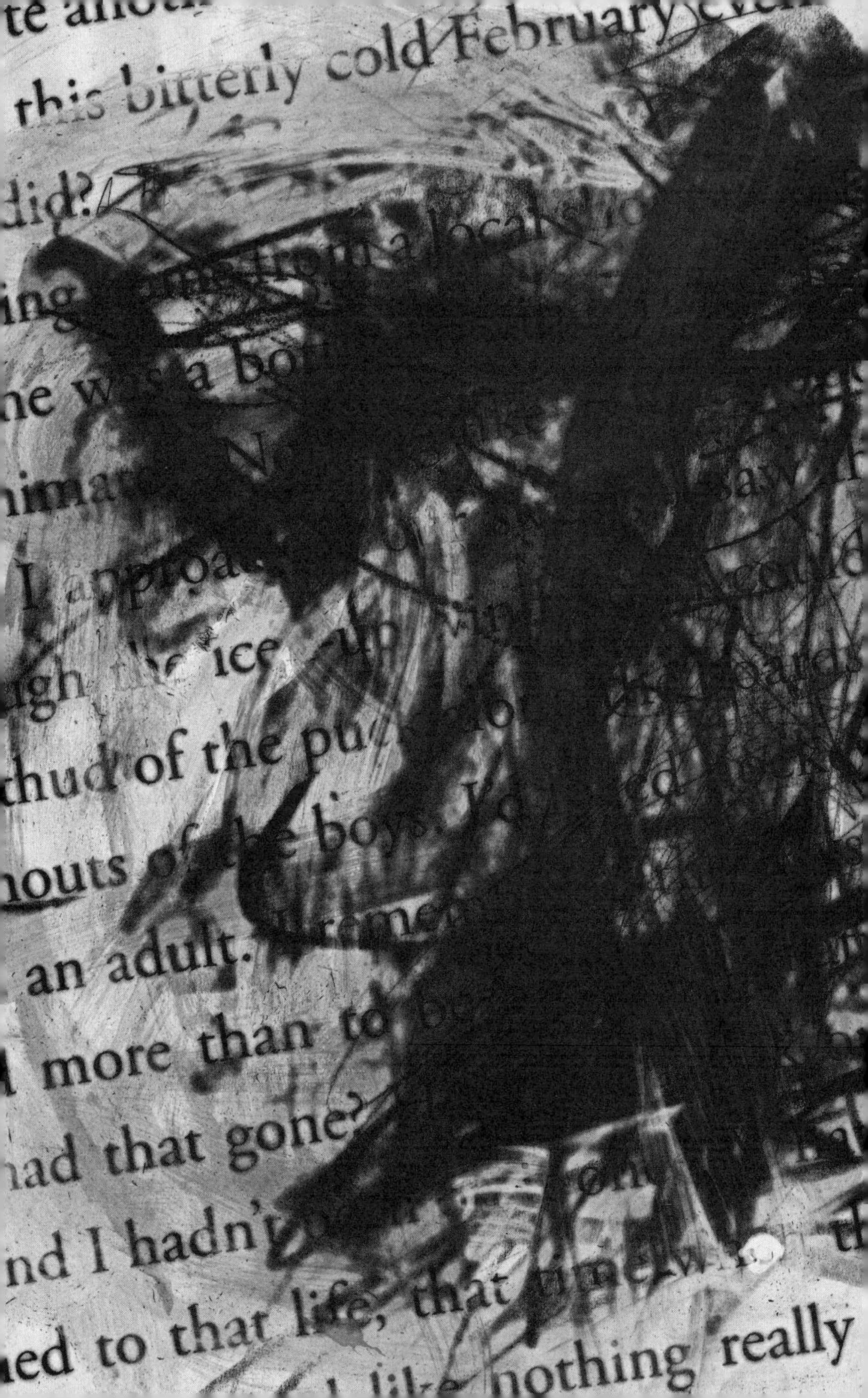
this bitterly cold February
did?
an adult.
more than to
had that gone?
nd I hadn't
ed to that life, that
nothing really

About a month or so after I saw Ryan in Montreal, I quit drinking.

I have no explanation for what went on that day. Certainly, my experiences with Ryan in 2000 had made me rethink my drinking. However, I'd be full of shit if I said he was the primary factor. But he was certainly a major player. Now, as I've said, I'm not religious in the least, but something crazy went on. How could it not have been? They always say that a person needs to hit rock bottom before they pick themselves up, but that was a bit of horseshit. I'd hit rock bottom quite a few times over the last few years. Hospitalizations, car accidents, fights, and many drunk driving moments where I'd have to keep one eye closed just to keep my focus. How those events didn't kill me is one thing, but *why* on earth I didn't change my life and quit drinking is quite another mystery all together.

So why on this bitterly cold February evening did things happen the way they did?

I was driving home from a local shopping centre. In the passenger seat beside me was a bottle of wine. I had an article to write about a Russian animator. Nothing like a little liquor to loosen me up for writing. As I approached our street, I saw the lights of the hockey rink. Through the iced-up windows, I could see the kids playing. I heard the thud of the puck along the boards, the whack of the stick, and the shouts of the boys. I'd loved hockey as a kid, but lost touch with it as an adult. I remembered the days when there was nothing I wanted more than to be out on a skating rink with other kids. Where had that gone? Here was a rink only two minutes from our house and I hadn't been on it once. What had happened? What had happened to that life, that time when there were things that made me happy? Seemed like nothing really made me happy anymore, nothing that gave me infinite, unadulterated pleasure or passion. I thought of how happy I was as that boy heading to the rink and suddenly a heavy sobbing sound burst forth from within me. I continued towards home and parked the car. But before I got out, I sat there momentarily, wondering what the hell had just happened and where it had come from.

Finally, I got out of the car and headed downstairs to my room. I opened up the bottle of wine and started working on the article. I knew at that moment that this was going to be the end of it. I would finish this bottle, but that would be it. The time had come to stop living in the darkness.

That very same day, some five hundred miles away in Toronto, animator Chris Landreth, who had served on the selection committee with Ryan, sent an email to a friend telling him that he was starting his new film about Ryan.

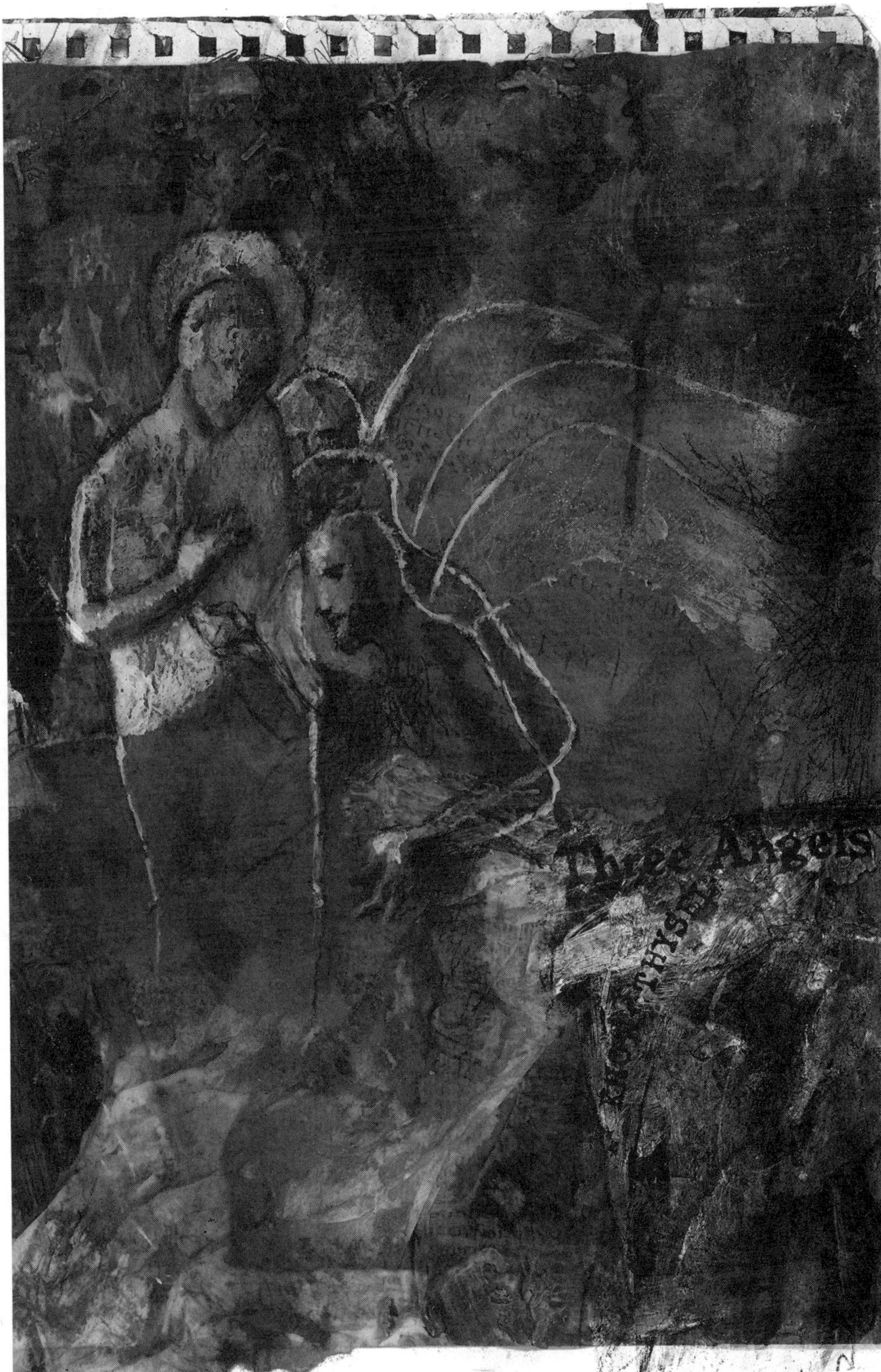
Three Angels

d mocked, ignored
and slowly
ety seem
herwise
ssage

Religion, which I'd mocked, ignored and condemned since I was a teenager, quietly and slowly reappeared in my life during the spring of 2001. Sobriety seemed to trigger it, but not in the ways you might imagine. Initially, it was pretty negative. First, there was Alcoholics Anonymous. I went a few times and just couldn't tolerate the religious element of the meetings. Sure, they denied that they were affiliated with any religion, but I wasn't comfortable holding hands and saying a prayer. I also didn't like the 12 steps that were the keystone of the A. A. "religion." They read like a sort of Ten Commandments (and indeed, they are taken from the Alcoholic Anonymous "bible" — otherwise known as "the big book"). Among the 12 steps were passages like:

> … came to believe that a Power greater than ourselves could restore us to sanity.
>
> … made a decision to turn our will and our lives over to the care of God as we understood Him.
>
> … were entirely ready to have God remove all these defects of character.

In my mind, I felt that I had caused my drinking problems. I didn't want God or anyone else assuming the responsibility for me. It was my shit and I'd deal with it my way.

It didn't help that I'd look around the room as someone told a horror story about their drinking days and see people chain-smoking or guzzling coffee. I went to only a few meetings, but always left depressed. My belief was that sobriety should make you feel good. I just achieved a minor fucking miracle in my life and I wanted to feel good about it.

A. A. wasn't for me, but it did work for others. The year I quit drinking I became intimate with two animators: Michele Cournoyer and Paul Fierlinger. Both had been sober for many years and credited A. A. with much of their success. Michele and I actually met one month after I quit drinking. In March 2001, I traveled to Austria to present a screening of Canadian animation films. This was my first trip sober. It was hard. I knew no one and, aside from my screening, everything was in German. I spent the days wandering around Graz, but mostly hid in my hotel watching bad old American TV shows from the seventies that were on in German. During one of the last days, I met Michele. She'd arrived late in the festival to introduce her potent film about addiction and sex called *The Hat*. It was one of my favourite films and I was excited to finally meet her. Being the only other Canadian, I was invited to join Michele for dinner with the festival staff and some Canadian Embassy people. We were introduced and, strangely, I felt an instant connection.

During dinner Michele noticed that I wasn't drinking wine like everyone else. She asked why and inexplicably I said that I was taking a break, but she knew I was lying and later, after dinner, while we were walking back to the hotel, I asked her why she wasn't drinking. She said she hadn't had a drink in almost twenty years. Relieved, I admitted that I also had a booze problem and had decided to try and stop.

After we returned to Canada, we exchanged many long emails and phone calls. Michele was very open with me about her experiences and beliefs. Just having her to talk to got me through so many dark and crazy days when a drink seemed inevitable. I even wrote an article about her films and life. She'd overcome many demons and was now a successful and happy artist at the top of her field.

The other pivotal person was Paul Fierlinger. He was also a proponent of A. A. We had discussed God a year earlier when I visited him. He described God as a sort of energy that's inside you. It wasn't some old guy with a white beard living on the clouds, but it still sounded weird to me. I just didn't understand this idea of energy being inside you. I kept thinking of electrical currents. Was it like the crazy guy who, a few years ago, shot down a TV sports reporter because he was receiving radio signals in his teeth?

Eventually I did go and see an alcohol counsellor. I met with him once a week for about two months. He was an intense guy, sorta reminded me of the writer James Ellroy. You just knew this guy had seen some bad shit in his life. I can't remember much about the sessions, but at the time they helped. I told the guy that I didn't want any god stuff and I didn't want to talk about all the stupid things I'd done. I just wanted to be able to get through the moment. He told me that the only way was to alter the way I was living the rest of my life. That seemed pretty complicated to me. How the heck can I turn around and change my entire life? How do I turn back the clock and make things all peachy in the snap of a finger? In the end, just going to these sessions helped. I stayed sober cause I didn't want to disappoint the guy. Figured he might beat the shit out of me.

The third angel arrived in May 2001 while I was attending an animation festival in Finland. While interviewing German animator Andreas Hykade, he told me about a feature he was making called *Jesus*. I was surprised to hear about it and asked if he believed in God. Without hesitation he said, "Yes."

He was using a couple of the fringe gospels as the basis for his story. One of them was the *Gospel of Thomas*. Andreas explained that the *Gospel of Thomas* portrayed a very different Jesus. As usual, I probably didn't show much interest at the time, but when I got home I immediately went out and got a copy. It turned out to be pretty fascinating stuff.

The *Gospel of Thomas* was, along with an assortment of gospels and writings, only discovered in 1945 in Nag Hammadi, Egypt. It was a lost gospel by someone known as "doubting Thomas." His words were an assortment of remarks and phrases he'd heard from Jesus. What was so remarkable about the *Gospel of Thomas* (as they called it) was that he gave a very different portrait of Jesus than the one I knew. Thomas' Jesus was not a long-haired, hippie messiah who preached the apocalypse, he was just an everyday guy, bit of a transient, who passed on good advice. He spoke directly to people about their lives. He told people to look within themselves for guidance and to reject the materialism and fraudulence of society. This Jesus doesn't speak about the kingdom of heaven being some mystical place in the clouds you go to when you die, but as something right here in the moment, something that's within you.

I read the *Gospel of Thomas* and Elaine Pagels' book, *The Gnostic Gospels*. I was fascinated with this idea of Jesus as this sort of wise guy, a man who traveled around saying smart things to people about how to find peace in their life.

I cracked open the gospel and was instantly struck by its similarity to the Pre-Socratic philosopher Heraclitus and also to Eastern religions. Jesus' words were presented as small fragments of dialogue. They were like anecdotes. But inside these minute passages, I found an array of words that knocked me on my ass:

> The kingdom is inside you and it is outside you.

> When you know yourselves, then you will be known, and you will understand that you are children of the living father. But if you do not know yourselves, then you dwell in poverty, and you are poverty.

> If one is whole, one will be filled with light, but if one is

divided, one will be filled with darkness.

One who knows everything but lacks in oneself lacks everything.

If you bring forth what is within you, what you have will save you. If you do not have that within you, what you do not have within you will kill you.

The last quote in particular caught my eye because I'd seen it in a poem written by one of my favourite writers, Nick Tosches. I always loved the passage and referred to it often. In general, though, these passages grabbed me because they seemed plausible. There were no outlandish Ed Wood-worthy scenes about virgins getting knocked up or dead people coming back to life. Instead, there was common sense. Here we have Jesus telling us that the kingdom of heaven is not some afterlife resort, it's something that you can find right here, right now. It's open to everyone at any time.

The other passages reminded me of the famous words of a temple in Delphi, Greece, location of the oracle and a sanctuary that was considered to be, literally, the centre of the world. In Greek mythology, Zeus sent a pair of eagles out from each end of the planet. The two met at Delphi. The oracle became a sort of shrine to Apollo. Pythia, the priestess of the oracle, was Apollo's earthly representative. As one story goes, Pythia's name comes from python. Apollo purportedly slaughtered a giant snake that released gas fumes upon its death. People would come to the oracle to seek advice from Apollo via Phythia. The priestess, in a trance brought on by the gas fumes that rose from the ground (apparently this signified Apollo possessing the woman), then offered cryptic, seemingly nonsensical responses that priests would later decipher for Joe and Jane Peasant.

More importantly, it was believed that there were three phrases inscribed inside the temple devoted to Apollo. One of the phrases was: "Know Thyself."

Two very simple words seemed to me to hold the answer to so many problems. Perhaps that's what Fierlinger meant when he spoke of God as energy. If so, then maybe this was an idea I could believe in.

* * *

I made it through that first year of sobriety, but it was not God, Apollo or Jesus who got me there. In fact, it was the words of a human in an email. I was about six months sober and not feeling much better about my life or myself. I wrote a desperate email to Fierlinger saying that sobriety wasn't working out and that I was close to drinking again. He replied:

Life can be rewarding without anything much happening but just experiencing peace of mind – hollow words for you if you're not experiencing it. Drinking will make you feel like a loser after a year and a half, but here's the BIGGEST warning: If you do pick up again, it's going to be much, much harder to stop than the first time. The novelty of discovering self worth for quitting will vanish and all that will come to your mind is that you can't do it. That's going to make you feel like a bigger shit and life will become a bigger mess than ever, because people around you will quickly agree with you that you can't stay off it.

Paul's words hit it smack on. For years I'd dreamed of being sober for a year. I always wondered what it would be like, but I never had the strength or courage to try it. I was so close to reaching that goal now. If I fucked with it now, the innocence or purity of that vision that was once a carrot to my jackass would be lost.

In Paul and Michele, I met two people who'd faced even more obstacles than either Ryan or myself and yet had somehow found the inner strength to overcome them. Since they sobered up, they were making the best films of their lives. I quietly wondered why Ryan was going to be the subject of a film and not them.

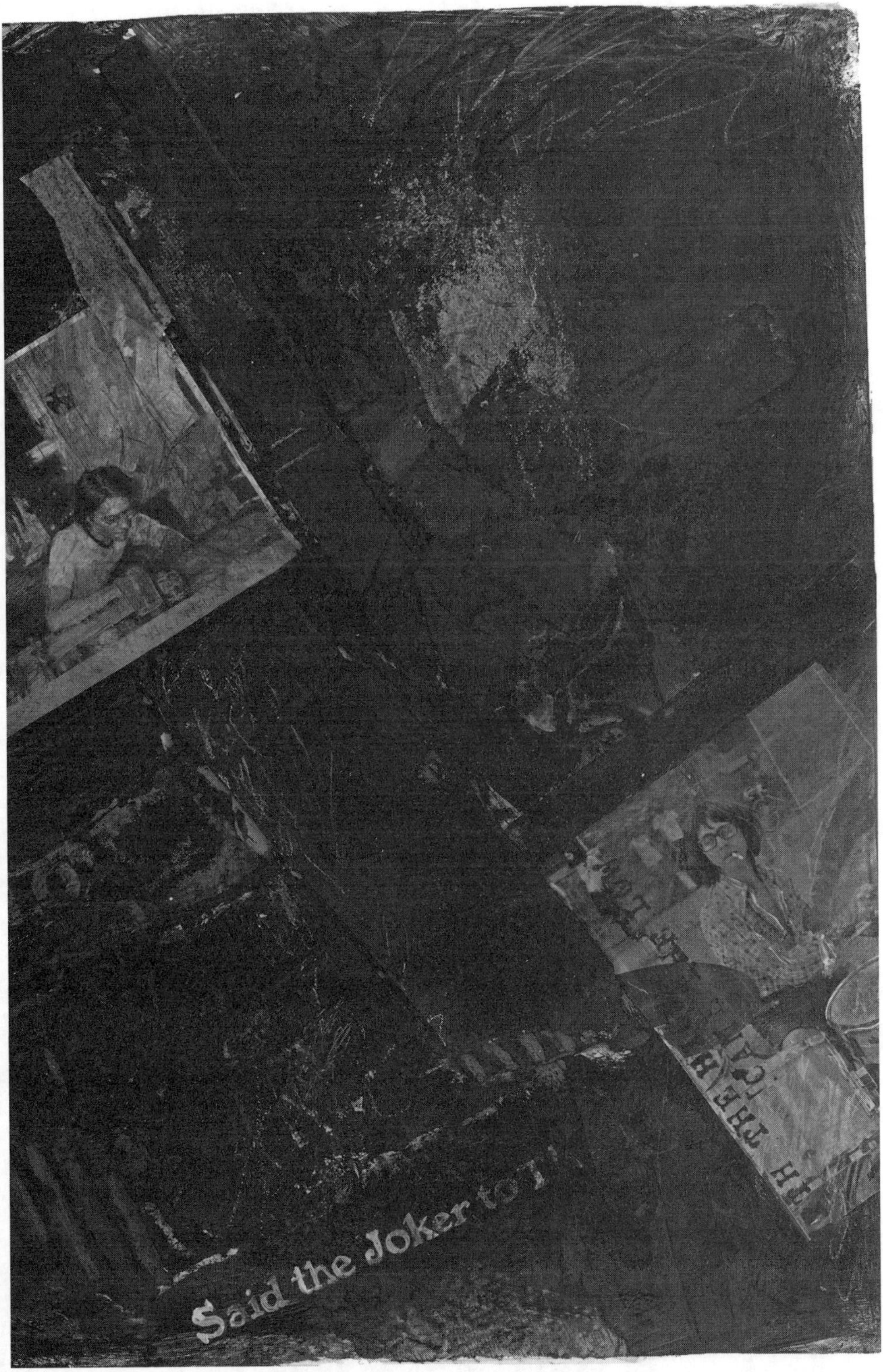
Said the Joker to

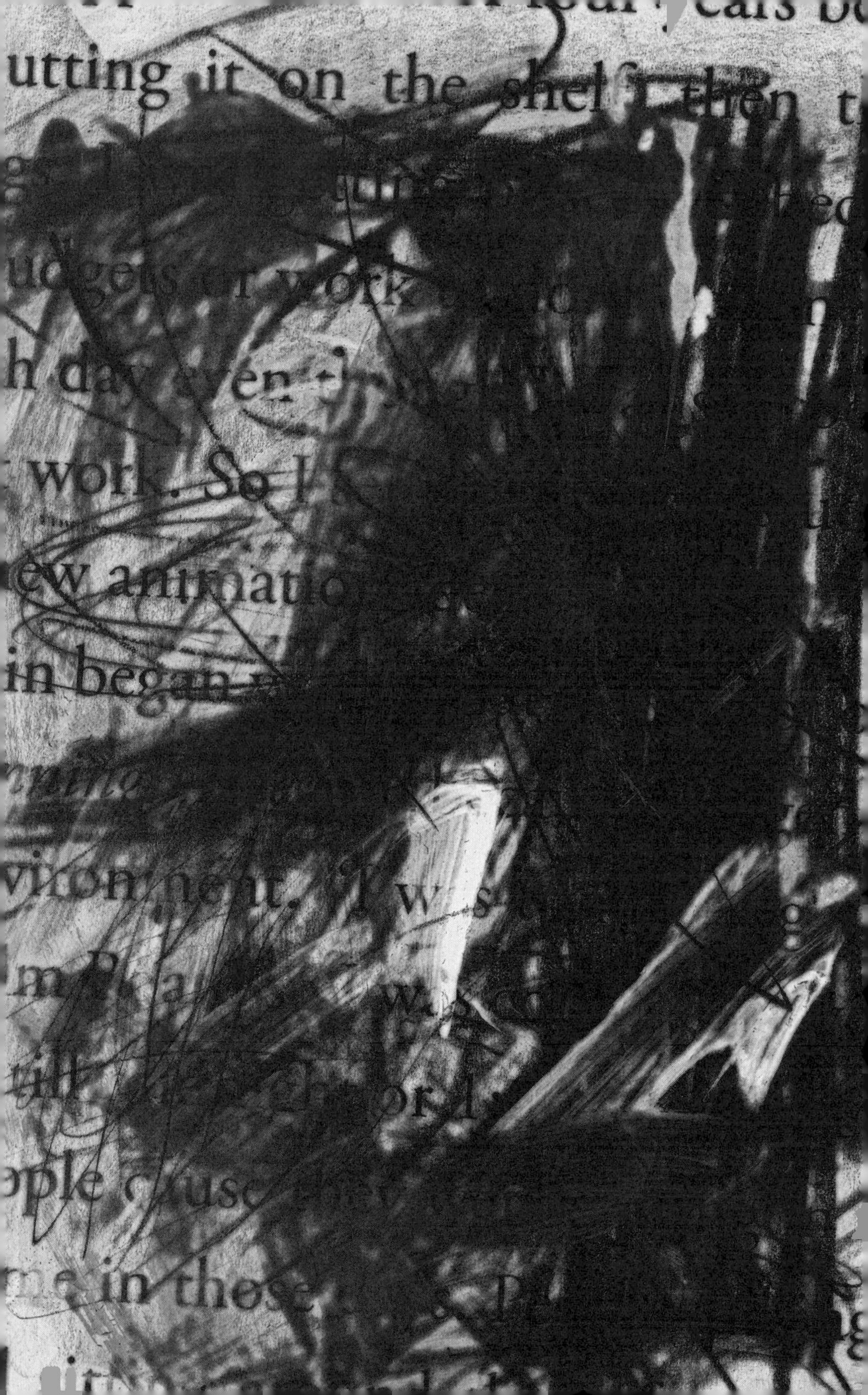
utting it on the shel
work. So I
ew animatio
in began
vironment.
ople
in these

Following *Street Musique*, Larkin was assigned to work on a feature film that the Board was producing called *Running Time* (1974). Along with the Dutch-born puppet animator Co Hoedemen, Larkin was asked to do three short animation sequences combining the actors with animation images.

However, *Running Time* soon turned into a nightmare for Larkin: "I was trapped into it for four years because the executive producers kept putting it on the shelf, then there were endless committee meetings. I was getting pissed off because I was on hold. I had no other budgets or work to do. I became totally without something to do. Each day even though I was still being paid by the project, I was without work. So I set up my own studio at home to try to come up with a new animation idea."

Larkin began working at home not only because of his frustration with *Running Time*, but because of a general disenchantment with the NFB environment. "I was trying to get away from the everyday life of the Film Board so I was coming in everyday around 4:00 p.m. and working till midnight or 1:00 a.m. just to avoid people. I started to avoid people cause they were getting in my way. There was so much wasted time in those days. People talking about the weather and the news and sitting around the cafeteria drinking coffee. I became a recluse, I guess."

Eventually Larkin set up a studio in his apartment. He worked out of that studio and ventured back and forth to the Film Board every few weeks:

> *I was trying to be an artist. They were not tolerating that I wasn't here from 8:00 a.m. till 5:00 p.m. I wasn't a nine-to-five guy and they were threatening to throw me out. I said, don't threaten me 'cause I think it's time for me to leave the Film Board. I've been there for twenty years [more like fifteen]. I had to get back to my roots as an artist, a sculptor,*

a painter. I got so fed up with working with film, all of its technicalities and budgets and conferences. There's too many conferences. When I approach a canvas with my paintbrush, there is no conference. I don't have to deal with executive producers. I just take my colours and [makes shadowboxing gestures] attack the canvas. And that's what I was when I was a teenager, just a beautiful artist, enjoying splashes of paint onto a canvas with my eye-arm contact that was so much more interesting. Once again, like when I quit school, I felt like a runaway.

So, with the Board's approval, Larkin worked at home on his next film, *Ding Bat Rap*, a project he anticipated would be approved by the studio. The situation was ideal for Larkin because, if he woke at 2:00 a.m., he could simply work on his film. This was something he couldn't do at the office. Larkin also notes that the producers knew that he was doing research and development for *Ding Bat Rap* at home while the feature was on hold. "That seemed to be okay with them since I was not able to work on the project."

Ding Bat Rap was to be Larkin's first "talkie." The film was to be set in a bar with a bunch of regulars sitting around talking nonsense with great earnestness. "A lot of people talk and talk without saying anything. They make gestures with their hands, give meaningful looks back and forth towards each other." Larkin had experimental voice actors to re-create the "babble." He had originally hoped to record actual dialogue, but noticed that people froze up, so he dropped that idea. (Larkin would later compare his idea to the bar scene in *Star Wars*: "I may be pushing it, but I think I was ripped off.")

He selected swing music for the soundtrack: "There was a beautifully organized music library at the Board, made to provide filmmakers with soundtracks for any subject. I selected that material and edited it myself. So I had edited my soundtrack, but I didn't have enough animation drawing. I had drawn my characters, about five. It was a very abstract, poetic thing. I had a storyboard and filmed still images, but there was no actual animation movement."

Thanks to new NFB English animation producer Derek Lamb, Larkin finally received a budget for *Ding Bat Rap*, but he continued to work at home. "I told my producers to trust me, I was working on the project, so they sent me my cheques." Larkin paid for the cab.

Larkin's producer, David Verrall (son of Robert), was given the task of bringing Larkin back into the fold. "I spent an exceptional amount of time and effort in trying to re-enable Ryan as a filmmaker here," Verrall recalls. "I went several times to Ryan's home on Park Avenue. I liked Ryan (as most folks did), admired his work, and sincerely believed he could turn things around." Verrall actually managed to lure Larkin back to the NFB building for a while by giving him access to one of the new animation cameras. Eventually, Larkin, either bored or stressed, would disappear for long stretches, only to be further behind when he re-appeared. In the end, Verrall reluctantly gave up.

Meanwhile, the programme committee was none too thrilled with Larkin's *Ding Bat Rap*. What Larkin saw as a satire on ethnic groups and nationalism was viewed with disdain as a reactionary, almost racist vision. "I was making sound and visual jokes against all people that were too full of pride. There was an anti-Muslim thing, an anti-Christian thing. I was trying to put down the nationalistic attitude that was happening at the time." Even McLaren backed out of Larkin's corner. "Norman was also sort of shocked by my heavy punk material."

* * *

A big factor in Larkin's increasingly discombobulated state was his addiction to coke. Coke was a big attraction to Larkin. It was a magical, almost spiritual experience that took him to worlds he'd never known. "The cocaine was giving me incredible insights into human behaviour and very acute sensitivities towards what constituted human behaviour."

Larkin claims that, during the sixties and early seventies, he only smoked hash and grass, until he gave them up when they made him anxious and paranoid all the time. Content with drinking beer, he soon became a caretaker for his mates. "All my friends were doing LSD and I was drinking my beer as I always do. And they were ridiculing me, 'you're so old-fashioned drinking beer.' They would ask me to take care of them while they were doing 24-hour LSD trips, to stop them from jumping out of windows and behaving in dangerous ways. I was taking care of a bunch of children experimenting with drugs. I was doing that for many years."

Larkin claims (as any good addict would) that he was using coke with respect and in moderation. "I was doing powdered coke and I was enjoying just the luxury of snorting in the most unusual places. I always had a little package and a straw and I would get into some situation and put my little powder in my hand and go [makes sniffing sound]. That became a thrill, a game. I was trying to prove something. Totally childish behaviour."

Later, Larkin started making his own coke. "We were cooking coke at home. You put it in a spoon and it makes crystals. I could smoke at home which was a wonderful experience except that the people who were around me kept coming into my house when I wasn't there and doing my coke and stealing my belongings."

But, contrary to Heraclitus' maxim, the way up was not nearly the same as the way down. With the high came the low. The neurological stimulation gave way to backlash. "It gave me a certain amount of energy and ideas, but the thing is that the ideas kept changing every few minutes. Every time I came up with a concept, another one would arrive. I was thinking too much and not doing. And I was also enjoying the thrill of it. Cocaine provided me with a marvellous sexual thrill, but it was neurological, an electronic sexual thrill, not the real thing. At the time I wasn't getting any sexual activity. I was getting it from cocaine. I couldn't even get my cock hard. It was a fantasy, a falsehood. Took me many years to figure that out."

Coke helped Larkin discover a confidence he never knew, but the pace of the magic locked Larkin into a fantasy world. A magician trapped within the allure of his illusions, Larkin was no longer able to work.

* * *

In Larkin's mind, he was making radical work for a conservative institution. But he also acknowledges that he was burning out. "I was losing my edge because I'd been there for too long. I was having a creative block that was probably the result of the coke." In a sense, Larkin was unable to grow up, or at least fit the model of maturity prescribed by the society around him. He was pushing forty, but living like a punk. He was playing in rock bands. He was still hanging out with younger people, financing their bands, writing lyrics. He was a godfather to the punks. Nevertheless, it was clear that Larkin and the Board were no longer good for each other. For Larkin, the NFB became increasingly restrictive. A coked-up, confused, talented Larkin wanted his freedom back; whatever the hell that was.

Larkin then stirred up more trouble when he was invited to create a mural for the NFB. What he drew was likely not what they had envisioned: an adolescent with an erection who may or may not have been ejaculating. The mural was 20 x 15 feet. "It was meant to be a satirical commentary on masculinity because at the time there was a year-long festival going on about women's rights. It was supposed to be comical relief from all their terrible, self-conscious seriousness."

It didn't matter. Ryan Larkin's tenure at the NFB was soon over. There was a modest effort to get him back on staff, and Robert Verrall regrets not being more stern with him. "Management and friends had tried, but Ryan was determined to go his own way. [I] should have read the riot act and insisted that he work in the environment of the Board; if it was good enough for McLaren, it should be good enough for Ryan."

It's not really clear whether Larkin was fired or quit. He claims he quit but there's no letter of resignation on file at the NFB. The only thing that is on record is that Larkin's last day as an NFB employee was July 29, 1978.

Larkin felt relieved to be out of the NFB. "I was no longer responsible for being a civil servant. I hadn't realized until that time that I was a civil servant. Then I became a freelancer, a free person. But having spent 15 years at the Film Board, I was not ready for the outdoors. I spent so many years as a spoiled child, and I wanted to change that, 'cause I knew about it and I thought, I'm gonna go out and try to make it was a freelancer as someone strong and beautiful.

"Evidently, I wasn't strong and beautiful."

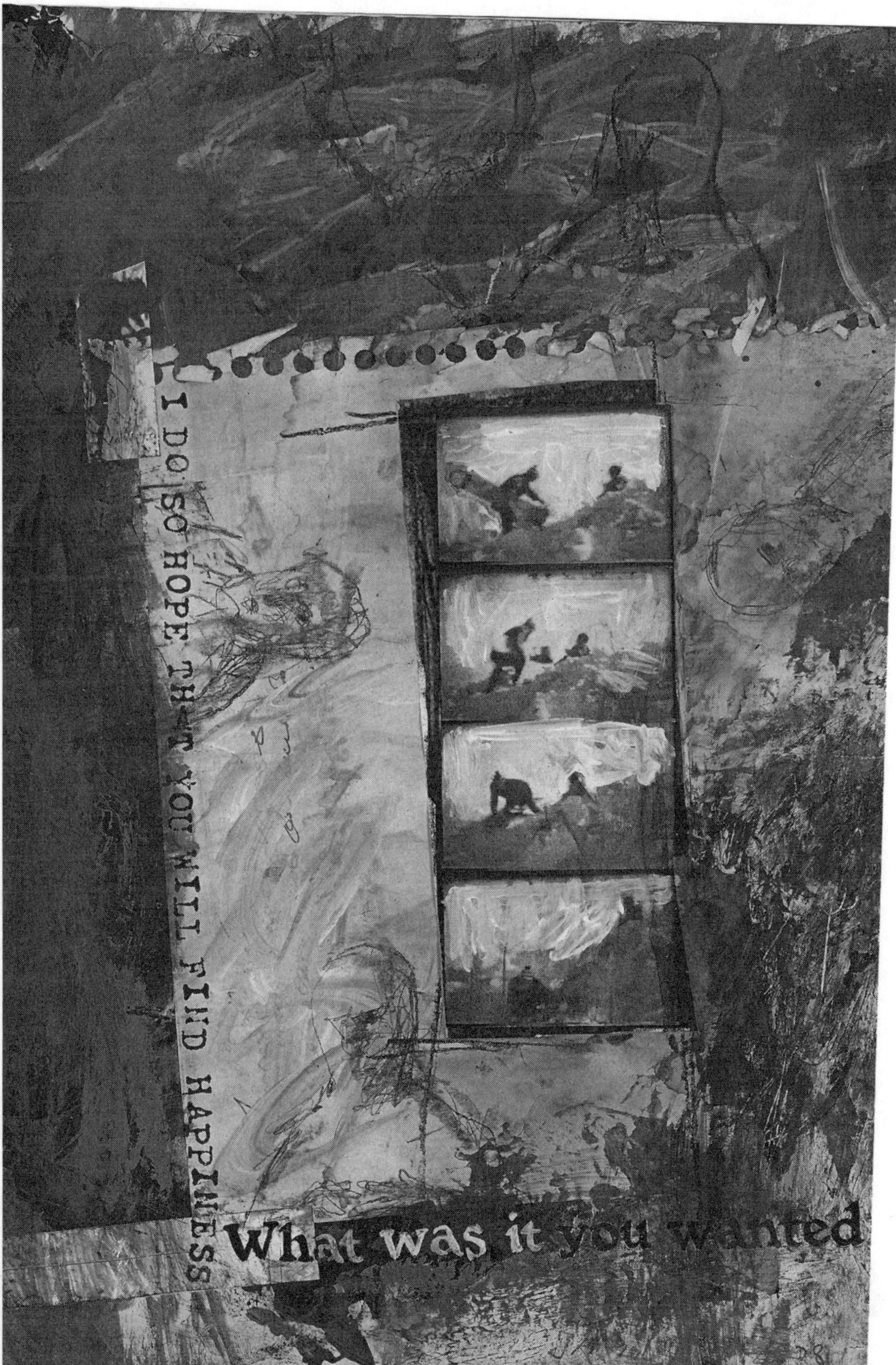
I DO SO HOPE THAT YOU WILL FIND HAPPINESS
What was it you wanted

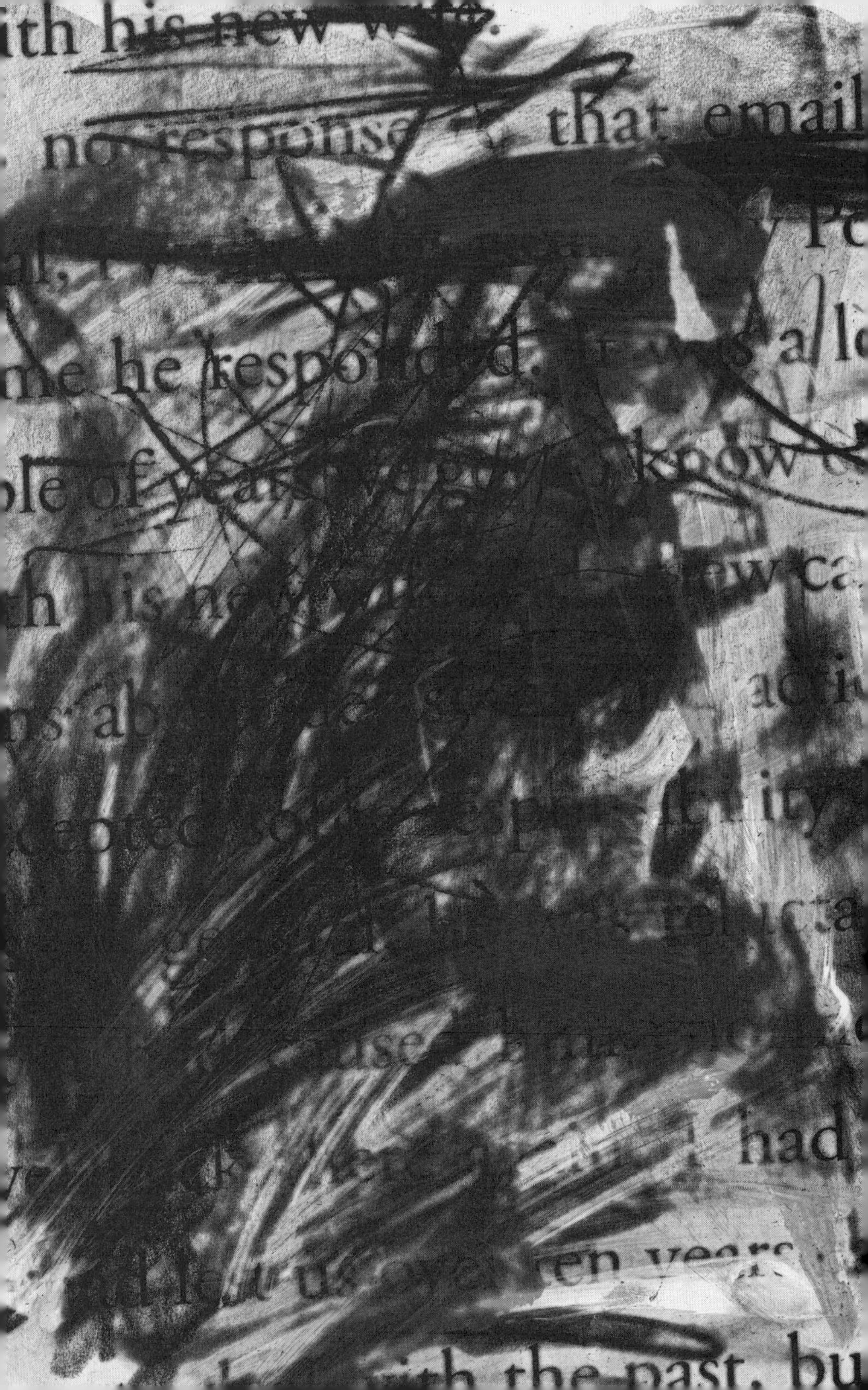

ith his new
response that email
me he responded.
ple of
know
had
ith the past, bu

That same week in 2000 when I met Biopops and Ryan, I had also gotten drunk and fired off a vitriolic email to my adoptive father. This was, outside of a flicker in the late 1990s, the first time I'd tried to communicate with him in over ten years. I knew very little about his existence now, except that he'd retired from the police and moved to the U.S. with his new wife.

There was no response to that email. Around the time of the Finnish festival, I wrote Not Really My Pops a slightly more subdued letter. This time he responded. It was a long, slow process, but over the next couple of years we got to know each other again. He'd found happiness with his new wife and a new career. Initially I pestered him with questions about decisions and actions taken when he was my father. He accepted some responsibility but refused to take it all on his shoulders. In general, he was reluctant to even address the past. He said that it had caused him enormous pain and that he didn't want to travel back there again. I had a hard time accepting that decision. He had left us over ten years earlier. It was nice that he had taken the time to deal with the past, but it was a shame that part of the cleansing didn't include his sons (my half-brother is his biological son). I should have cut it off there, but I didn't. I was so desperate to find a father. Maybe we could make it work this time.

It didn't quite work out that way. I can't blame him at all. I rushed into the room (just as I had done with Biopops) without really considering the consequences and possibilities. Over time our families got to know each other. Not Really My Pops visited Kelly, Jarvis and me in September 2001 (where we watched the events of 9/11 unfold before our eyes). A year later, our trio went to visit him and his wife in California. They seemed quite happy together. I felt good in their house. His new wife was the polar opposite of my mother. She was perky, encouraging and loving. Clearly, Not Really My Pops had changed his life around.

I came to understand that Not Really My Pops had made poor decisions largely because he decided to stay in an unhealthy marriage. He did this for the sake of his sons. I don't think he realized that keeping the marriage intact would only make the bruises deeper. My anger towards him began to fade, but the psychic scars remained. I quickly realized that the hate was just vanishing into nothingness. I simply did not feel any love for this man. Forgiving aside, there was no love in our house. How was I supposed to find an emotion that wasn't there to begin with? So, after the rubble of hate had been cleared, I was just left with one big assfull of emptiness.

After I told Not Really My Pops my real feelings, he wrote me a disappointed but sympathetic response:

It is unfortunate that you carry a cloud around with you, it must feel terrible. I came to Ottawa really hoping that we could build a renewed relationship. I also came to Ottawa guarded that in some way you were not truly ready for it. I enjoyed my visit with you nonetheless. It was good to see you.

As a writer you choose your words well in your writings. Maybe it was still a little early for us to have been together but only you could have known that. As I have said before, people must move on and not dwell continually in the past. This is something that your mother never could learn either. I on the other hand have learned through all of the adversity that I have seen and been part of in my life that moving on is the only answer. Moving on is probably the only thing that can help you remove that cloud, I do so hope that one day you can achieve that goal. Absolutely no one will be able to change you or help you to change until you are ready to do so.

Please take care of yourself and your family. I do so hope that you will find happiness. Good luck and work at it.

He was right. I hadn't moved on.

Not Really My Pops had always scared me, and that feeling hadn't left during our brief reconciliation. He reminded me of characters like Fred Flintstone and Tony Soprano, but mostly of Robert Mitchum in *The Night of the Hunter*. This dark, brooding powerhouse of a man who was shadowing your every move, not to protect you, but to harm you. When he came to visit, that shadow had returned, as did the scared little boy. There's a scene near the end of the film where the boy clenches his stomach as he watches his stepfather — who has murdered the boy's father and mother — being arrested in the same manner he saw his biological father arrested at the beginning of the film. He's now witnessed the "death" of two fathers. Despite loathing this stepfather, the boy feels a sickness in his stomach. He's once again alone.

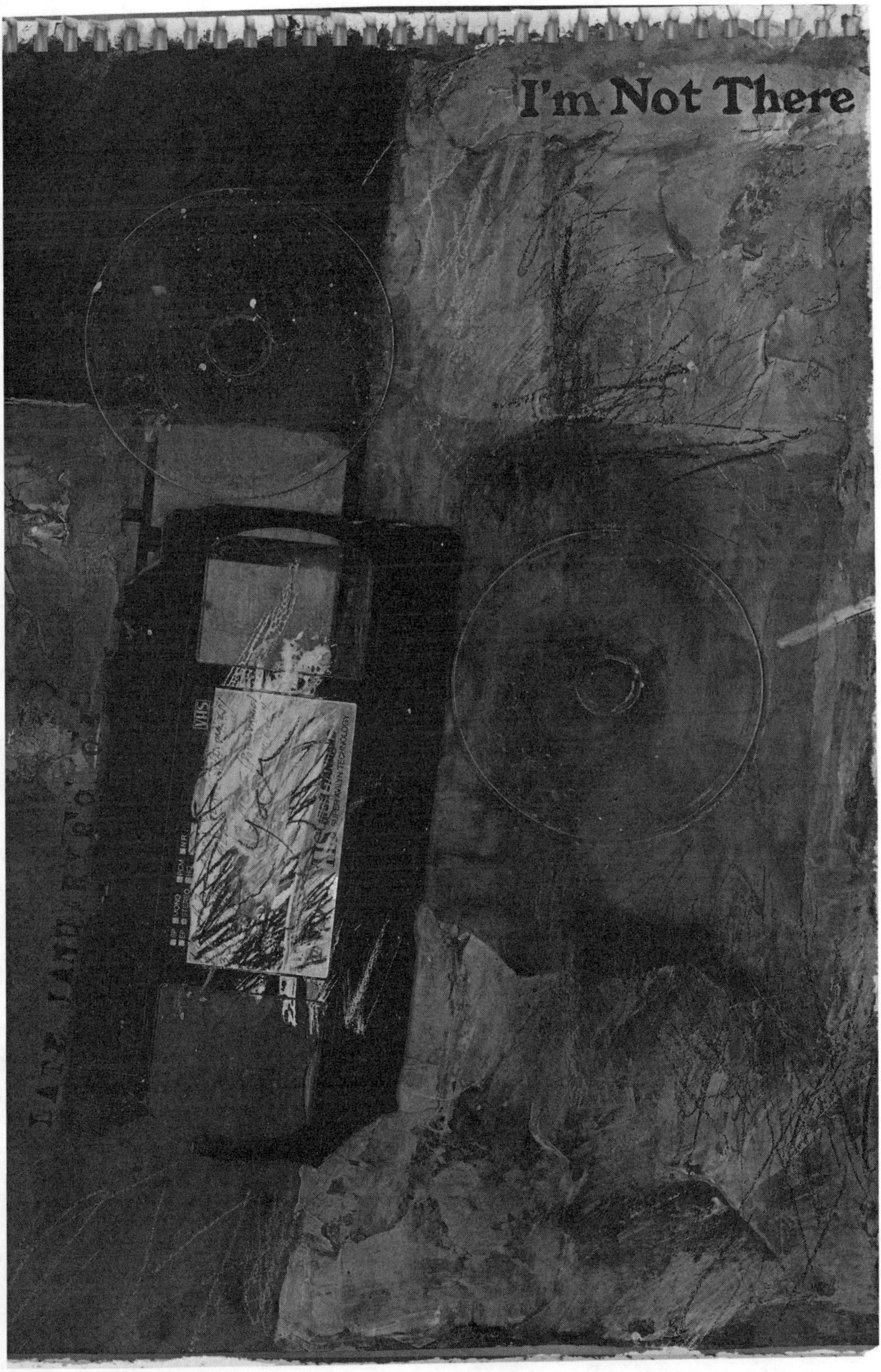
I'm Not There

ow Ryan, actually

on the selec

Animation F

s ation

in ro

d this un al

tho ur would

Ch

got to meet ill

In late January 2004, a courier arrives with a package. I open it to find the word "Ryan" scribbled on a VHS tape. It was from Chris Landreth. He's finally finished his film about Ryan.

Like me, Landreth had been touched by our strange encounters with Ryan in July 2000. As Chris explained it to *VFXWorld* in 2004:

> I had come to know Ryan, actually, from kind of an accident. I was asked to be on the selection committee of the Ottawa International Animation Festival. There were originally to be four of us animation professional types selecting films. At the last minute, one of [them] dropped out. The organizer of the festival, Chris Robinson, happened upon Ryan Larkin in Montreal. Chris had heard of Ryan, and that Ryan had this unusual lifestyle of panhandling for spare change. He thought it would be interesting, in light of this other guy dropping out, to have Ryan be on the selection committee. So, Chris drove Ryan to Ottawa from Montreal, and that's how we got to meet him.
>
> That week was very unusual. It was basically three of us, being the animation professionals, judging these films, and Ryan was at that point acting very much like a person who had not been around animation at all; very much like a bum, actually. He was saying, "I got to have my beer now... I'm tired, I got to lay down..." He was out of it for the first day or two. Then something kind of remarkable happened. He came to realize, I think, that he was in the company of people like he had been around when he was a creative person, and he started to really come alive, and we got to see him being lucid and engaged and very impassioned. That transformation of the personality was a very striking thing.
>
> Then the last day, we showed each other our films. Ryan was the last, and he showed *Walking* and *Street Musique* and another film called *Syrinx*. We had seen the film *Walking* before, but now we were really looking at it. We came to realize that this person was a flaming genius in his time.

> We were looking at him today — and, first of all, what a change, what an incredible contrast... and then, second of all, as Derek [Lamb] in the film says, he's living out every artist's worst fear. But if this is where he's come to, there's something that's actually not horrible about that. There's something very redeeming.
>
> I was immediately inspired to try to get that story into a film. I sat on that for a few months before acting on it. Then I decided that's what I wanted to do.

Landreth hooked up with Larkin again during the festival in September 2000. "While we were on the bus over to the [animators'] picnic I asked him, without any real premeditation, it was actually quite impulsive. He was on the bus with me. I said, what if I made a film about you, based on what I've known about you since I met you? He said, 'Sure.' But I did nothing about that until February 13, 2001."

In February Landreth approached Copperheart Entertainment producer Steven Hoban, who he'd worked with briefly on an IMAX project called *Cyberworld 3D*. "I remember," says Landreth. "He produced that, and wanted to include *Ryan* in that film and re-render it in 3-D — stereoscopic vision. [H]e was overruled… but we stayed in touch, and he was completely on board from the very beginning, along with this other guy, Jeremy Edwardes. And a month later, I visited Marcy [Page] at the [National] Film Board. [The NFB came on board as co-producers in late 2002].

During the spring and summer of 2002, Landreth headed to Montreal and spent over 20 hours conducting videotaped and audio interviews with Larkin. Other than knowing that the film had to be Larkin being interviewed, Landreth didn't really have a specific direction at this stage. "The idea was vague at first," he says. "I was thinking along the lines of Nick Park's *Creature Comforts*, in which he interviewed people at a zoo in Bristol and then fashioned an animated film around the interviews."

Then came the turning point. At one point during the interviews, Landreth brings up Larkin's alcoholism. Chris tells him that he saw his own mother die from the disease and that he doesn't want to see Larkin follow the same path. Larkin, who'd been drinking heavily during the interview and was pretty much obliterated by this point, gets worked up by Landreth's question to the point where he explodes in anger. "It's obviously a big subject in Ryan's world," Landreth told *VFXWorld*, "because he acts so impassioned and angrily toward it. But it is also a big subject in my world, too, and because of that, it brought the interviewer (me) way more into the story than I would have planned beforehand."

In March 2004, I wrote about the film for my Animation Pimp column in *Animation World Magazine*:

> In the film, Landreth uses Maya software and does an extraordinary job re-creating himself and Ryan as characters in the film. The interview between the two takes place in an old, run-down cafeteria that looks like the waiting room for hell; an assortment of disfigured and, literally, broken characters occupy the space. Ryan's appearance is initially horrifying. Landreth has re-created him as a fragile, incomplete person. We see the remains of what was once a face and much of Ryan's body is twisted, busted or just not there.
>
> As Ryan reflects on his life, Landreth uses animation to create spaces and give psychological depth to the characters that simply would not be possible in live action. In one poignant scene (and there are many — including the moment when Landreth pulls out original drawings from *Walking* and shows them to an emotional Larkin), we meet Felicity, Ryan's old girlfriend. Seeing the two of them speaking "face to face" about what might have been is powerful, heartbreaking stuff.

> When Ryan places his hand on Felicity's, I dare you to keep your eyes dry. His memories of their happy times together momentarily turn him into a younger, "complete" Ryan, with hippie threads and long hair, who comes to life in his award-winning film *Street Musique*. He is filled with joy and soon begins dancing with his creations.
>
> Perhaps it's because of my intimacy with the subject, but I found the aforementioned alcohol scene difficult to watch (and I mean that in a good way). At one point, Landreth (now wearing a halo of sorts) brings up Ryan's alcoholism. Ryan, the calm, reflective, scared little boy, is caught off-guard. He claims that his beers are all that he has left. He doesn't want to become a tea drinker. Landreth tells him that he just wants to see him stay alive and return to filmmaking. Suddenly Ryan erupts. He stands up and takes on the appearance of a demon with red spikes protruding from his face. Ryan berates everyone and no one for his state. Everyone had robbed him and without money he has nothing. An intimidated Landreth backs off, his halo explodes and he wonders why he prodded Ryan to begin with.
>
> The scene is powerful, mature, and tense stuff; something you don't see much of in animation these days. The combination of Landreth's inventive character design, fuelled by the raw awkwardness that you could only get through a real, unscripted interview, gives this scene an intensity that is rare in animation. *Ryan* offers no affected, grand philosophical musings, no soppy poetic histrionics. This is life with all its dank, dark, dirty warts. This is the story of a real life gone astray. I don't mean just Ryan's life either. Landreth is drawn to Ryan because he sees aspects of his own life and family in Ryan.

Ryan is a film about failure. There is no happy ending. Landreth realizes that Larkin will not change and the film ends with Larkin back working the street. But there is a glimmer of hope; Ryan may not have changed, but by knowing him, he seems to trigger change in others. "In some ways," says Landreth, "I look at his life, and there's something very reassuring about it. He's basically followed Murphy's Law [if something can go wrong, it will] as an artist. If you look at his life now — yeah, he's poor, he's sort of on the bottom rung of society — but, on the other hand, he has in many ways a very positively structured life. He has a community of dozens of people who, if they don't know that he is an artist, at least know that he's a decent guy, and they take care of him. He has a community of people that a lot of us would find enviable."

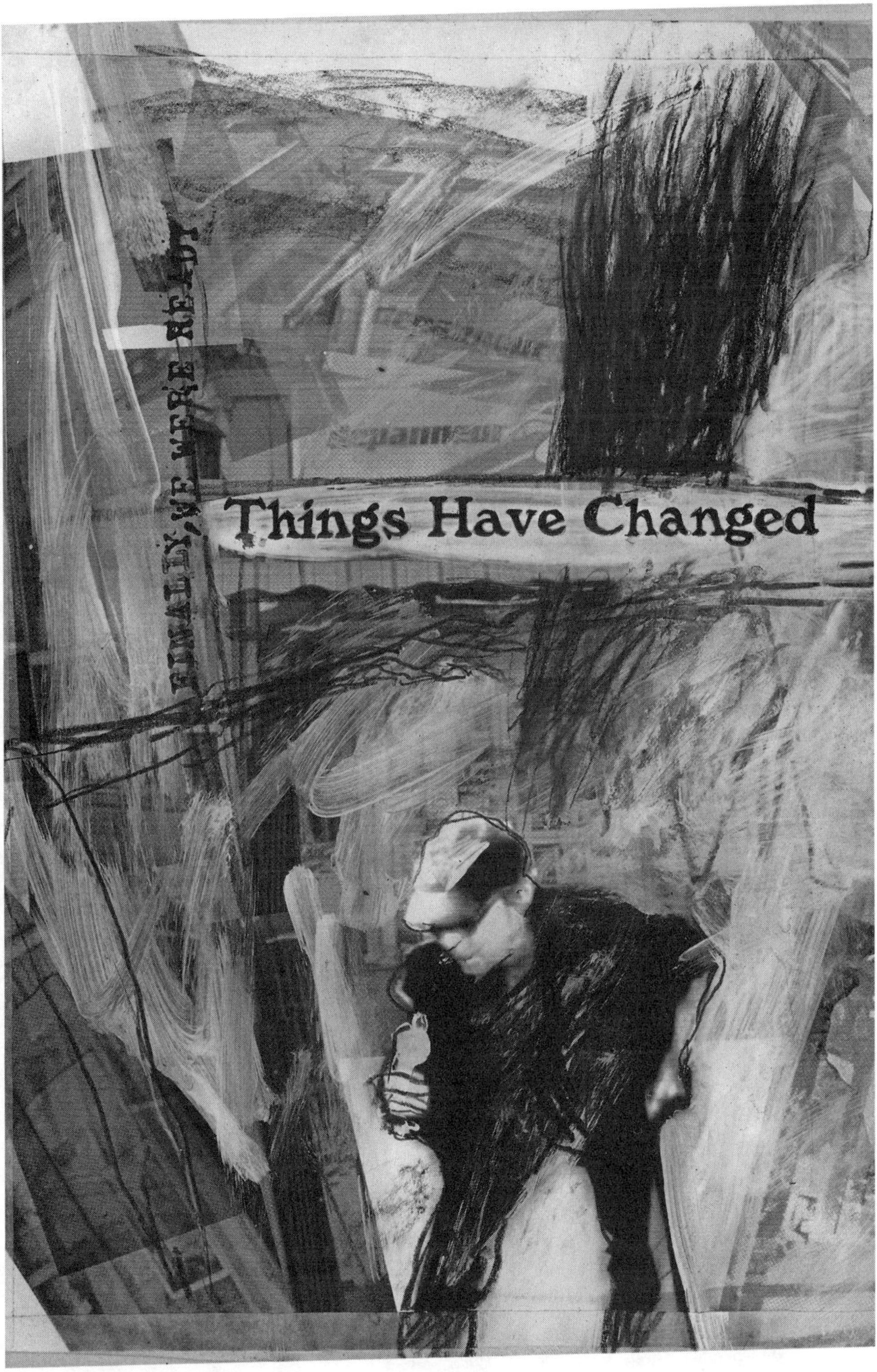
FINALLY, WE WERE READY
Things Have Changed

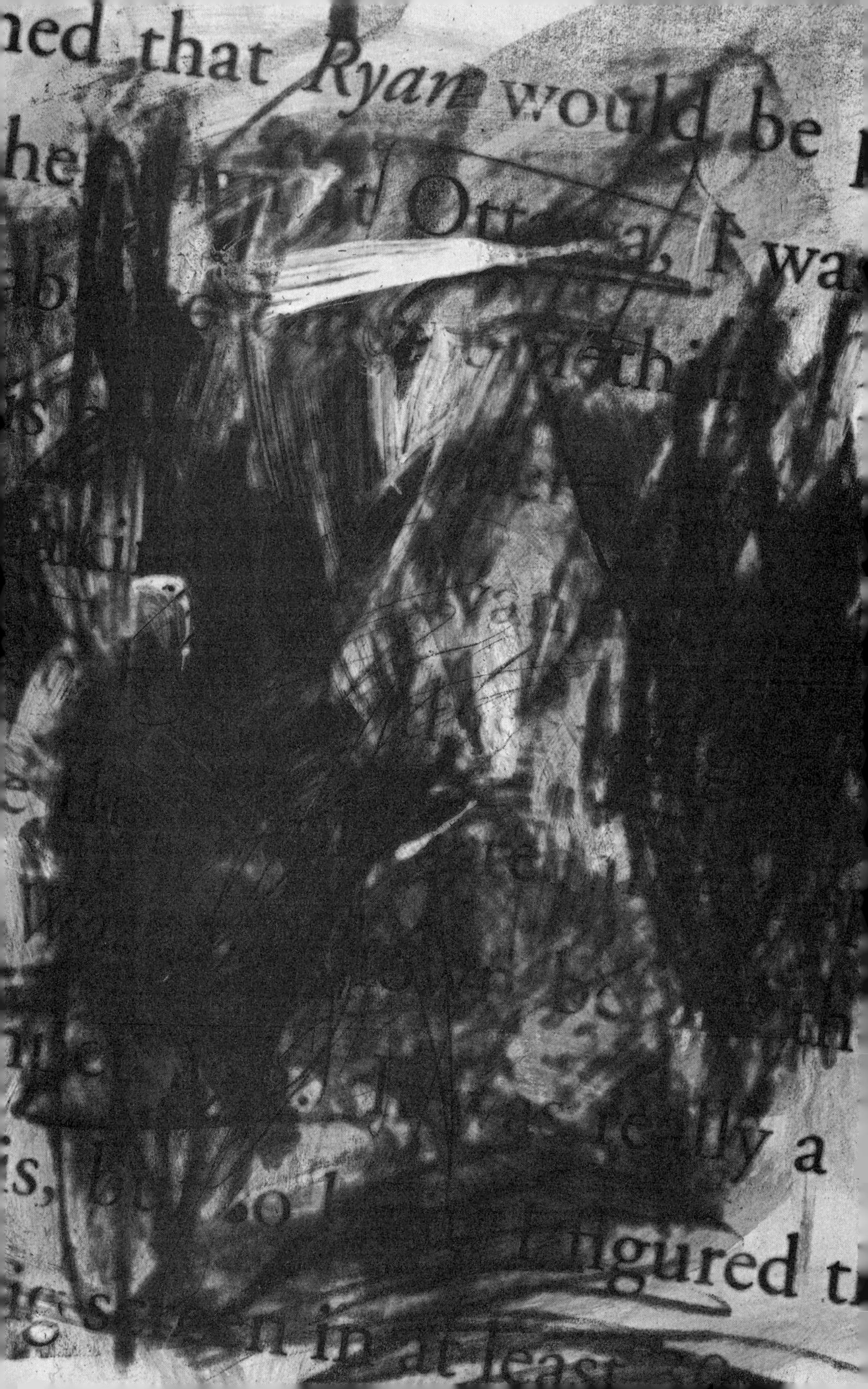
ned that Ryan would be
igured
in at least

When I learned that *Ryan* would be premiering at the Cannes Film Festival, rather than at Ottawa, I was pissed off. Still, I knew that we'd still be able to offer something special. We'd have the real Ryan again. By this point, my interest was no longer in helping Ryan or his cause. I was taking full advantage of the publicity I knew we'd get from having him here. If this was gonna be business, then I'd play along. To make the whole screening a special event, I arranged to have Ryan's film *Walking* shown before the screening of *Ryan* in the Friday night competition. It was really a bit unfair to the other competitors to do this, but so be it. I figured that Ryan likely hadn't seen *Walking* on the big screen in at least 30 years. It would make the night extra emotional for him. The publicity would be fantastic.

First, though, we had to get Ryan here. I called him a few days before the festival to ensure that he was coming. He said he was, but, typically, he wanted someone to pick him up and insisted that I accompany the driver. Sure, I have nothing better to do a day before the festival. But I agreed because I didn't want to blow this promo opportunity. Before I hung up, he also told me that he was concerned about media interviews because his face was in a bit of state. He said that he was just walking down the street when a group of guys called him "faggot" and then, apparently, beat the shit out of him. I figured there was more to it. There always was with Ryan.

"Don't worry about it," I told him. "We'll make sure you look like a dapper young man again."

Petr, the festival driver, and I went to get him a day before the festival. Sure enough, he wasn't ready. It took him about 20 minutes to gather whatever it was he needed. And he looked bad. Half his face was bruised. They'd really given it to him good. Ryan finally came out… but… now he had to go find his pop bottle. He was still storing the damn thing in a parking lot across the street. Retrieving the 7UP bottle took another five minutes. Finally, we were ready.

Wait up, not yet. Ryan requested that we stop off at the store so he could pick up some drinks for the road. He seemed sure he wouldn't find this brand at an Ottawa store and begged us to stop at this convenience store off St. Laurent St. I've never encountered a snobbier fucking drunk. We zipped up St. Laurent and Ryan led us to the store. We waited outside while he went in. Time passed and Ryan still wasn't out. It was about 15 minutes by now. What the fuck could he be up too? We couldn't find parking, so we were partially on the sidewalk at the side of the store.

"I'll go see what's up," I finally said. I walk in and see Ryan carefully pouring all 12 or so beers he's bought into plastic containers. Surprisingly, the storeowners didn't seem to care. Seems like Ryan was a regular here.

"Ryan, how much longer are you gonna be? We gotta get going."

"Uh... yeah... sorry, man…" he stuttered.

"You could do this in the car, ya know."

But no, he couldn't. Turns out it wasn't just about keeping everything in plastic… but he also wanted to get the refund on the bottles. Finally, after about another 20 or so minutes, we were on our way back to Ottawa. Ryan seemed okay in the van. He was funny and pretty clear. He asked about old staff members. Had an amazingly sharp memory when he wanted to. I told him that most of the staff had moved on. He had a good sense of humour still too. When we discussed his bruises, he said that he worked it all out. He was gonna tell people that the bruises were from the reconstructive surgery he had done after making the film. (Remember, the "Ryan" character in the film barely has a face or body left). The rest of the drive was pretty uneventful except when we had to stop at the Ottawa airport to pick up a Korean friend/guest. His English was lousy and he was a relatively posh guy. Now he found himself in the back of a van with a smelly old guy with a purple eye. He must have wondered what the heck he'd gotten himself into.

Overall, Ryan was relatively easygoing and more comfortable, but, truth be told, I was glad to get to Ottawa and drop him off in his hotel. I always felt tired after hanging out with him. It was like taking care of a slightly off child.

After we got him into the hotel, he wanted to be sure that I hooked up with him later. I assured him that I would. I lied. I met a couple of guests for dinner and decided that there was no way in hell I wanted to deal with Ryan again that day. Later, after I checked into our staff hotel room, I found a message on my mobile (which I guess I had turned off) from him. He was freaking out that I hadn't called him. He was swearing and threatening to go home.

This was new to me. Ryan seemed a bit more self-reliant four years earlier. I ignored the call and decided to call him first thing in the morning. Deep down, I was already having regrets about bringing him here. I was stuck now. I pushed for him to come and he was my responsibility now.

Fortunately, the Film Board had sent a P.R. guy. I didn't like him that much. Actually, he was okay as a person, but he was a P.R. guy. He was there to do his job, which was to plug the shit out of the NFB and, especially, Ryan. That made him a bit of a weasel in my book. Still, he was a valuable asset. I figured if he wants to promote Ryan, I'd make him earn his money. He can also babysit Ryan. It was the only way, really. Landreth wasn't coming till Friday and I couldn't very well saddle Petr with this detail. He had driving jobs to do and it wasn't fair to put the burden on him. Basically all I cared about was getting Ryan through the Friday night screening. After that, he could fuck off.

By the day of the festival, we had developed a routine. Someone would meet him in the morning (he didn't get up till late morning though) and ensure that he had a supply of beer and smokes. Then we'd take turns escorting him to screenings or hanging out with him while he drank. It was a precarious situation. We needed the booze and smokes to keep him from freaking out, but if he had too much to drink he became a mess of a being.

Chris arrived Friday morning to give us all some relief. It was unfair really. He didn't invite Ryan. He was here as our guest, to enjoy the celebration of his film and the festival itself. I admitted to him that I was overwhelmed. "I had no idea he was this bad," I told Chris. If I'd known Ryan needed a constant caretaker, I never would have invited him. I hated Ryan for making me feel this way, but not enough to turn away a chance at a national TV spot that came around on Friday morning.

We first had to wake Ryan and see if he was up to doing a TV interview. No, it wouldn't be live. Yes, he could use the joke to explain his bruises. Yes, he could have a few beers to soothe his nerves. In the end, it took us at least two hours, maybe more, to get the interview going. By then I wondered what I was doing here. I was just riding his failure like everyone else now. I didn't care about saving or protecting him. I just used him for us. We sat outside our building on a brown picnic bench. The day was unusually warm. As I listened to Ryan spout the same bullshit about why he stopped making films, and art in general, I found myself increasingly depressed. I just wanted everyone to leave. Larkin drained whatever energy I had left right out. I felt tired, impatient and confused. Was it the guilt of knowing I'd become just like everyone else? Just resorting to using the man for his failed life, or was it something that I wasn't able or willing to admit to myself because it would force me to realize that my life was good and that I was actually happy and stable?

Four years earlier, I had admired Ryan. I wouldn't say I wanted to be like him, but there seemed to be something honourable about his apparent defeat. He provided me with a cover for my own crumbling life. Well, my life wasn't crumbling anymore and watching Ryan's pathetic performance, one that had become worse since we first met, made me angry at myself and at him for not changing, for not seizing, as I had done, the fucking opportunity that was presented to him.

We got the interview. We got national TV coverage. There were our three faces reaching all across the country. Little did I know it was just fuelling the fire and feeding the myth.

I sat with Ryan during the competition screening. I felt a little of that old energy come back. I wanted Ryan to be moved when he realized that his film was going to open the evening. I realized that it was a risk, that maybe he'd be overwhelmed by the sounds and images of the past. Deep down, did I want that? Did I hope that maybe it would slap him out of the dark?

When the film started, I could hear him grunting in the dark… then I heard a stream of swearing: SHITFUCKPISSCOCKSHIT-FUCKPISSCOCK. A chill ran through me. Oh shit… I've made a terrible mistake. This is gonna be a nightmare. But then I felt his hand touch my arm. Through tears, he said, "Um… thanks, man… I wasn't expecting that… thanks, man. It's beautiful." Then he fell silent and lost himself in the film. Occasionally he'd grunt or say "shit" or "wow"… but mostly I watched him let himself be carried back to his life… or maybe it was a wish to lose himself, literally, in the images of the film. Did the world make more sense back then? Was it easier for him to coordinate the world and the mess of emotions that travelled in his head? I felt the anger subside. Clearly he was on an enjoyable little trip. Whatever his choices, his life was nearing an end (the way I saw it). Why not give the guy something good? Even if it's an illusion, it's something. It's all.

As if seeing his own film wasn't enough, now he had about 30 seconds to recover before the film about him appeared. This was the first time he'd seen it on 35mm film in a theatre with an audience. He mostly stayed silent until a bit in which Felicity says that Ryan's dad had apparently been violent towards him. "That's a lie," he yelled out. "My father never did anything like that." It was a strange moment. Was it true? Certainly he'd never mentioned it to me during our interviews. That doesn't mean it didn't happen. But Ryan was extremely sensitive. Could it be he said something in anger at the time to Felicity? Maybe things weren't as bad as they seemed? I thought of my own son. He's extremely sensitive. He sometimes say he wishes he had another family and things like that. He doesn't mean it, of course, but I sometimes wonder if later on he will construct emotions in his head… and convince himself that we/I did something horrible to him.

Could I have over-exaggerated the past? Maybe things weren't as bad as they seemed. It makes me doubt my past. And what if I'm wrong about the past I thought I lived? If everything I constructed before me was a lie, then where am I now?

The film ended. The spotlight fell on Chris Landreth and Ryan. Ryan savoured the spotlight. He bowed and pretended to tip his hat. We left right after the film. Chris and his girlfriend took Ryan back to his hotel. He was clearly overwhelmed by the short evening. It was probably best to get him out before he was hounded by eager young animators who had come to worship him.

* * *

The next day was the worst I've experienced at the festival. I got saddled with Ryan most of Saturday evening (after Chris babysat him during the day). He was already in one of his states and heavily drunk. His lips were quivering, face twitching. He was ranting to no one in particular about "Negroes."

I asked him if he wanted to eat. He wasn't hungry, but he'd like a drink. So I dragged him along with a couple of friends. One of them, an American animator who'd just done a film about a sculptor, was clearly excited to be around Ryan. I introduced everyone to Ryan. Ryan, naturally, perked up and put on a little show. "Enchanté, mademoiselle. Good afternoon, sir." I used to get a kick out of it. Not anymore.

We crossed the Rideau Canal overpass and headed for the nearest pub. I wasn't interested in seeking out anything fancy. Ryan was in a potentially volatile state. I was hoping we could neutralize him for an hour and then I could drop him off on someone else. Didn't quite happen that way. As he stumbled across the bridge with his walking stick now the only thing keeping him up, he suddenly unzipped his pants and pissed on the sidewalk. People passing by tried to give off that look of feigned apathy, but you could see the disgust creeping from their lying eyes. We waited for Ryan to zip up and continued on our merry way.

"Ryan, couldn't you wait to find a fucking washroom? It's broad fucking daylight here." He just laughed. He didn't hear a word I was saying. We reached a fake British pub and sat on their plastic patio. Figured that was safer. We could get him out of here fast if need be, plus he could smoke. There were other people from the festival there and you could see that Ryan really created a buzz. People were whispering and making motions with their eyes. This was Ryan's moment to shine. He was being given everything, but he was, literally, pissing it away.

He calmed down a bit once we sat down. One of my friends inadvertently saved the day by asking Ryan questions about his films and life. Ryan loved talking about himself, so that seemed to make him happy and sober him up momentarily. A Swiss colleague, the director of another animation festival, was remarkably cool around

Ryan. No show of disgust. She actually felt a lot of sympathy for him. "Chris, you're too hard on him. He's really suffered, you know. Look at him. He's very much alcoholic." I nodded my head in agreement, not because I agreed with her, but because I was too tired to argue anymore. Everybody loves Ryan.

Dinner was tense. Ryan kept getting up to piss—on the sidewalk. I figured we'd get kicked out, but maybe the waiter was scared. Ryan was getting a little louder. We'd foolishly let him have vodka. He usually just drank beers, but for some reason he insisted on something harder. I let him, figuring it would buy me a few minutes of peace and perhaps tire him out. But it didn't. Soon he started twitching more frequently and pounding his first on the table.

"What's wrong, Ryan?" someone asked.

He went on about how uncomfortable he was here and how he needed to get home. This was the last thing I wanted. This film had a chance of winning the grand prize and I wanted this pathetic little fucker up there on stage when they announced his name. I'd endured his behaviour for five days now. He wasn't going anywhere. Of course, I lied to him and said, "It's too late for today, Ryan, but see how you feel in the morning. I can ask Petr to take you back. It's no problem. How about another drink?" Ryan, naturally, accepted. All thoughts of leaving were, for the moment, drowned.

After we finished our food, we headed back towards our office. The American animator wanted to show Ryan his film. I guess he figured that Ryan would find some solace in a film about another screwy artist. Along the way, Ryan started talking about the animator's Asian roots in a pretty derogatory manner. "Are you a Chink or a Nip?"

"Neither, I'm Korean."

"All the fucking same," Ryan mumbled, his face growing increasingly ugly.

He then went off on an unexpected tirade about immigrants in

Canada. The usual rant about "them" taking jobs away, they were lazy, shiftless and that sorta stuff. I had no idea where this came from. It was very strange to hear this within a festival environment. Most of the animators — except some of the Eastern Europeans I knew — were all relatively liberal people. Maybe it was Ryan's working-class roots. He came from a relatively uncultured background and was often intimidated by his more worldly colleagues. He also repressed his sexuality, at least early on. His attraction to his colleagues, like McLaren, was partially because they were homosexuals. He was attracted to them, and undoubtedly they were hot for Ryan (who was a good-looking guy in his youth). But for years he controlled the urges and lived with a variety of women.

Maybe this attitude grew from the street. I can't even imagine the people and things that Ryan has encountered on the street, but if his bruised face was any indication… he'd been involved in a lot of bad stuff. We only really knew the clean side of his hobo lifestyle. It was almost like the Charlie Chaplin version. We saw the hidden beers, the "spare change" routine, and the affable tramp. We didn't see the beatings, the blowjobs, and the shakes, or being fucked in his dirty ass by strangers. We saw hints of Ryan breaking down and I always felt that he was real close to offering to suck my cock for $10, but somehow he managed to keep it together. Maybe this is what made him crazier in these situations. He had to put a bit of a front, no matter how flimsy. He had to at least pretend to have some hold left on society's rules and regulations. This is why he wanted to go home so much. On the street, in the mission, he could be free. There were no pretences anymore. Identity vanished. I'm sure it wasn't all so dark. Ryan was also a very shy person. He liked people, but he liked being on his own.

To his credit, my Korean colleague just ignored Ryan.

I was steaming though. The more I repressed myself, the more I wanted to kill Ryan. But I just walked faster and said nothing.

We took Ryan up to our office to show the film. I stayed outside. I needed to grab hold of myself again. The last thing I wanted to do was snap before closing night.

To my surprise, Ryan actually stayed awake and told my friend how much he loved the film.

We all sat outside on a picnic bench for a few minutes before Ryan started up again. He was moving into psycho territory again; pounding his fist, swearing, his face convulsing more. "FUCK. I'll kill those goddamn Jap fuckers." He was slurring his words heavily now. We could hardly understand half of it. I didn't want to understand any of it. At this point, I called a driver to take Ryan back to his hotel.

For the next 10 minutes, I sat silently. He was ruining the whole week. I just wanted Ryan to go away. But I couldn't do it. I needed him too much.

* * *

The last day of the festival is always stressful. I have to collect the winners list from the jury, get their statements, work with staff to select the films we'll screen for the "Best of" programme that night. And then choreograph the awards ceremony. It was good to be busy because it kept me from seeing Ryan all day.

As we approached the start of the awards ceremony, I was stunned when one of our staff had a breakdown and started berating me. He accused me of bailing on the festival, of not giving a damn about it. In a way, he was right. I was totally disconnected from the festival. But it wasn't all me. I didn't anticipate having to co-babysit Larkin. I ended up skipping screening introductions and panels I was supposed to moderate so that I could take care of him. But in a way,

I wanted that. I just wasn't into the festival anymore. I didn't feel like I belonged. I didn't know how to draw. I didn't really love animation all that much. It was just a job I stumbled into after university. I guess I'd let the alcohol convince me that there was something more, that I really did want to be here. But now I wasn't so sure.

Meanwhile, Ryan was still grumbling about leaving. By now I knew that the film had won the Grand Prix. There was no way he was leaving just yet. I tell the NFB publicist so that he can prepare a release, but he pisses me off by telling Chris Landreth. He tries to justify it by saying that it's because of Ryan's presence, that they need to prepare him or figure out what to do with him. Bullshit. Ryan is better off *not* knowing, because, if he does, he'll get antsy and want to drink. Then he'll keep drinking and come award time, he'll be loaded. But hell… if it keeps him from leaving, so be it.

All went well in the end. The ceremony itself was awful. The jury members were too casual. They screwed up names. One jury member's English was so thick that no one actually knew who won the award she announced. Then when it came to the Grand Prix, the award's sponsor came up. She was drunk and completely misread the page. I had to quickly step in and re-announce it to the audience. After that it was all fine and dandy. Landreth came up, put on a good show, said the same things he'd been saying at every other festival (and who can blame him) and then he called Ryan up to the stage. The audience went nuts. Ryan bowed and curtsied and flashed his strange-looking grin that seemed half Stan Laurel, half Tommy Chong. He loved it. Briefly, I saw him close his eyes. For a split second, he found his paradise.

The next day, before Ryan left, I asked if I could speak with him. I told him that his drinking was really bad and that he was killing himself. Initially, it was a bit contrived, like I felt an obligation as a reformed boozer to say something, but, as I was talking, I really felt quite genuine. "You're gonna kill yourself, Ryan. You'll be dead very soon if you don't stop this. Do you want that? Look around you. Look at what has happened to you the last five years. People want to help you. People love you. They want to see you back on your feet, making films again. You had an effect on these people. You touched them. You've been given this bizarre opportunity to turn things around. It pisses me off that you can't seem to grasp that."

In Landreth's film, Ryan EXPLODES with rage when Chris tells him to stop drinking. I'm a bit worried that I'll get screamed at too. But it doesn't happen. Ryan is calm and he seems genuinely moved. All he says is: "Don't worry, man. I'm gonna be okay." I feel good. We embrace and he heads home.

Ryan held off from drinking during the drive home for about 10 minutes.

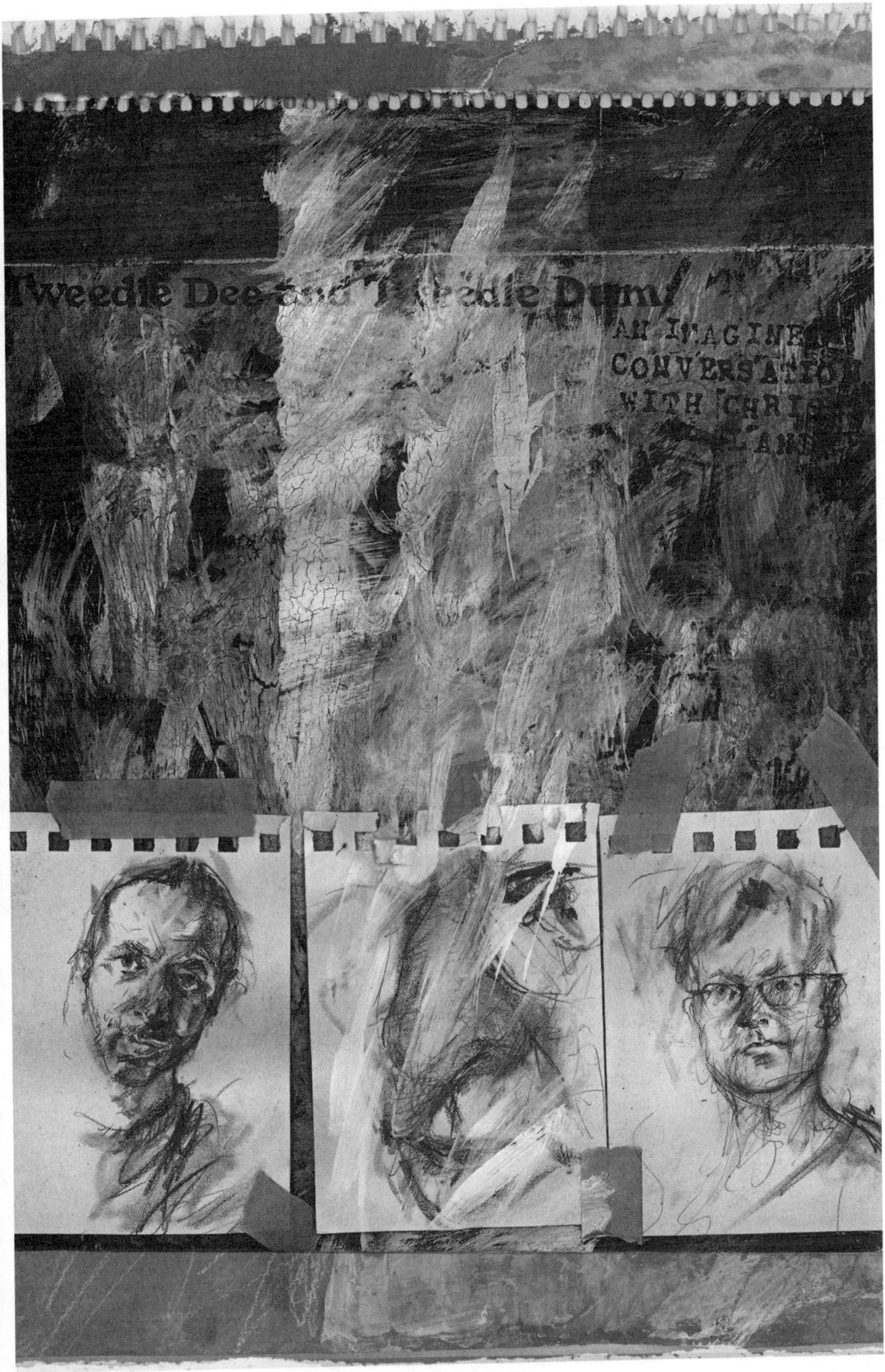

ly just interrupted me and said
ts to help Ryan
with
all
e's only
ity ... this film has p
as now ... but
a chan
Chris saw his m
delivers the goods
y ... hey
fronted his
solve and
in t
not ready
not judging
BUT the image of Chris in the
n face, resembling Ryan, followi

In the fall of 2004, I wrote a negative article for *Animation World Magazine* about my negative experiences with Ryan at the 2004 Ottawa festival. I also took a few shots at Landreth's film, which I'd become increasingly disenchanted with:

> I'm not so sure about Landreth's film anymore. Maybe it was a week of hanging out with the real Ryan that changed me. Kelly just interrupted me and said, "Maybe everyone just wants to help Ryan." Yeah. Maybe. I don't think anyone involved with all this is out to hurt Ryan… I too believe that we all want to help him… get him [on] his feet... but there's only so much that we can do. He's had ample opportunity… this film has put him in a position where he has options now… but until he stops chuggin' black labels, it ain't gonna change. Yeah… also… so where was I? I have no doubts about Landreth's intentions, but I think he made the wrong film. Chris saw his mother in Ryan, but in the end, he didn't deliver the goods there. The film IS called *Ryan* so technically... hey… that's okay... but I don't believe that Chris really confronted his demon. He's clearly got some mother pain to resolve and he just didn't do it in the film. But hey, maybe he's not ready yet. I'm not judging or slamming him for that… BUT the image of Chris in the end on the street with broken face, resembling Ryan, following Ryan's path… just doesn't add up because of this. It's not earned. Chris isn't honest enough about his own fears and demons to make us really believe that he might very well end up on the streets with Ryan.
>
> Ok. Yeah… it's an inverted world. We're inside Landreth's head. I know. I get it. But there are other things too. We don't really get a good grasp on why Ryan has "fallen." We're led to believe that alcohol is the main problem… but little is mentioned about Ryan witnessing the death of his brother as a teenager. I still believe to this day that that tragedy and the subsequent, unspoken, negative reaction of the family to Ryan played a big role in where he is today. Not to mention some definite personality disorder issues.

> Ryan feels unfinished… incomplete. Don't get me wrong… it's a good, very good film about the fragility of identity and definitely merits the attention and acclaim its getting… but I think we me and you all need to sit back, take a breath, some distance and get some perspective. Anyway… enjoy, embrace and applaud Landreth and the real Larkin, But hey, do the same for Fierlinger, Cournoyer, Drouin, Hoedeman and the many, many other people who overcame demons or just learned to live with or without them. No, they're not heroes, but neither is Ryan.

Chris phoned me after reading the article.

"I read the piece."

"And?"

"Why are you so negative about all this? Can't you be happy? Can't you see the positive in this story? You really don't have much faith in Ryan, do you?"

"Are you blind, Chris? Did you not see the same guy I saw this year? The one who was shaking, quivering, and freaking for beers. The guy who pulled his dick out in broad daylight and pissed on the streets. He wasn't doing that four years ago, at least not around us."

"He was just nervous. He spends his day doing his own thing and being at a festival; being obliged to be somewhere is just something different for him. And even though he didn't show it, he was worried about how the film would be received, how he'd be received."

"Chris, if we were talking about a 16-year-old, it would be one thing, but this is a 60-year-old man. The guy is never going to stop drinking and you can't see that."

"You don't have enough faith. I've put aside all the prize money in an account for him. We've got technical support ready for him once he finishes this storyboard and is ready to do his next film. Who knows, maybe he'll be ready to get a place of his own soon."

"I would love to be wrong, pleased to have my foot stuck right down my throat, but you're living in a dream world. Ryan couldn't survive on his own before, when his health and mind were relatively better. How the fuck do you think he's gonna manage now? He couldn't even handle being on his own during the festival. Do you really think he's gonna suddenly settle into a nice studio apartment, work all day, pay the bills on time, go for dinner with the neighbours? It ain't gonna happen. He's too far gone."

"I have faith in him."

"Blind faith. He won't stop drinking and no amount of fucking faith is gonna change that. If anything, we've done more damage to him. Now he feeds off the hype. He just wants your money, your beers, your smokes, your fucking chicken wings. He ain't interested in being saved. He never was. He isn't your mother, Chris. It's as though you're trying to reach your mother through Ryan, but it's not gonna bring her back. Look, you made a nice film, you've got all sorts of attention and fame now. Just enjoy it and take advantage of it so that you can be happy."

"Why does this bother you so much? You wrote your stories; you got attention for the festival. I don't understand why you are so obsessed with this story."

"Because it's become something I didn't want it to become. Lesya and I just wanted to give the guy a space to save himself. We realized pretty quickly, though, that he didn't want that. But now your film has turned him into some icon of the disenfranchised. Everyone is running around pretending they want to save him. It's just doing him more damage, it's turning a guy who is a loser into a damn saint."

"Chris, first off, a saint doesn't need to be saved. I wasn't trying to save him. I made a film about artistic failure, about a guy who got pushed to the edge and fell over, just like my mother. Like you, I saw my own life in there. How could I not?"

"That may well be, Chris, but that's not in the film. The film you made is phony. It's like reading the *Gospel of John* with all that horseshit about Jesus walking on water or being "the true light that enlightens everyone..." In the end, you show no understanding of addiction, and I don't think you have come to terms with your mother by doing this film. You didn't have the guts to really explore yourself and her. Hell, you don't even try to understand how Ryan got to where he is. Your film is like reading the Cliffs Notes on addiction."

"Okay, Doubting Thomas, but do you think that just because you've overcome addiction that you're the spokesperson, that only you know the deep dark secrets of addiction? You made this whole story about you. It was never about Ryan."

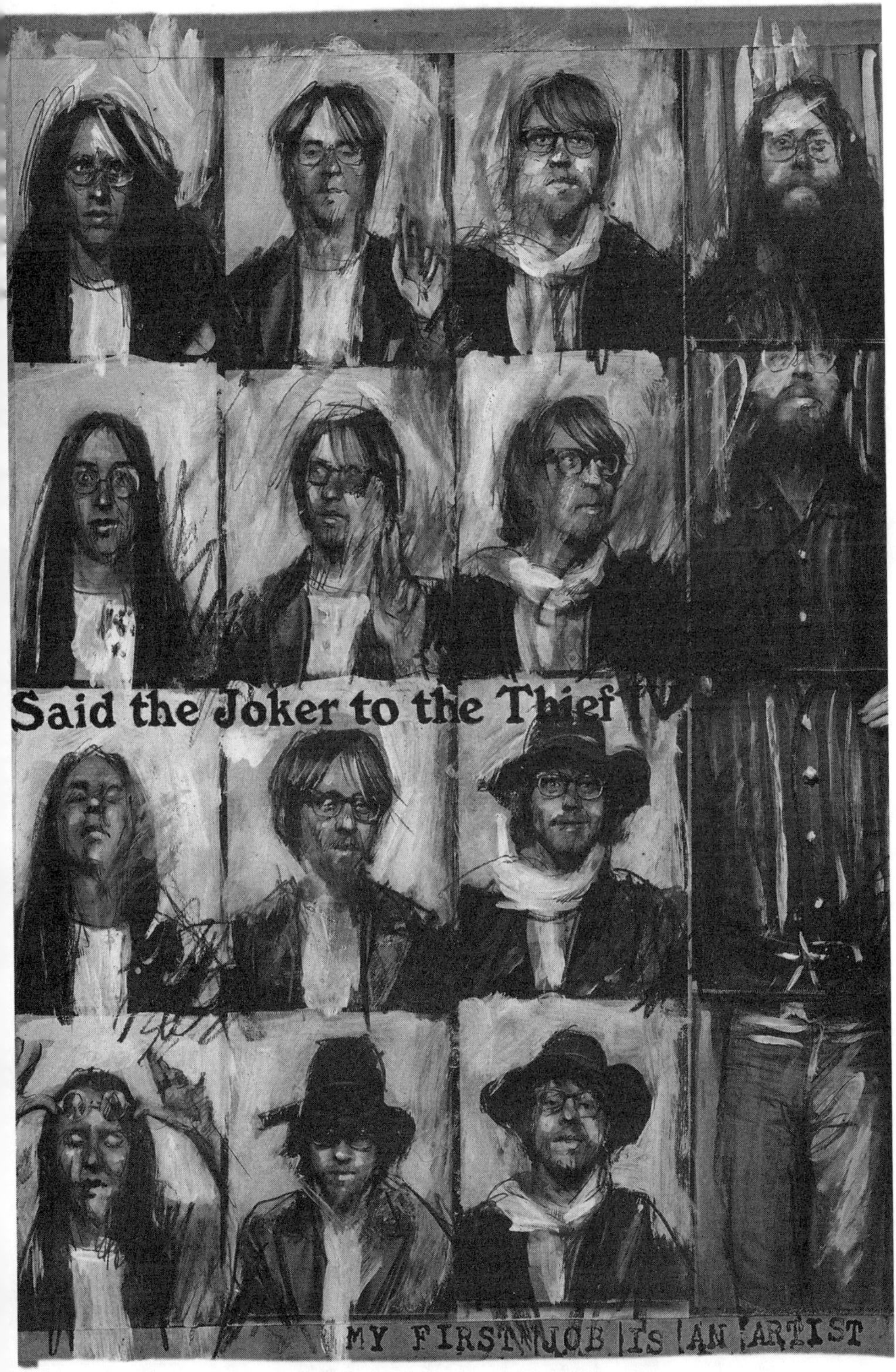
Said the Joker to the Thief
MY FIRST JOB IS AN ARTIST

ort time as
on his head an
tches. The nex

Freed from the stifling environment of the NFB, Larkin was convinced by his girlfriend at the time that he should work on commercial feature projects. (Odd advice, given Larkin's experience with *Running Time.*) Nevertheless, he headed to Toronto where he worked for a short time as a storyboard artist at Nelvana. Larkin worked for two months storyboarding the final sequence for the feature film *Rock and Rule*. Unfortunately, he wasn't around to see if his work made the credits (it didn't). One night Larkin was working late, probably snorting some lines and sippin' on some beers, when something fell on his head and knocked him out. He ended up in the hospital for stitches. The next day, Nelvana quietly and quickly put Larkin on a train bound for Montreal.

It's not really clear what happened, but Larkin admits that his girlfriend would come around at night, he was still doing coke, and he was rarely without a drink in his hand. Unlike coke, Larkin accepts his drinking condition with the greatest of ease; in fact he claims it makes him healthier. "I've been doing it ever since I was a child. When I was ten, the doctor told my mother that I should drink one or two beers a day to put on weight. I'm an alcoholic, not a drunkard."

In 1980, young animator/artist Joe Gilland was looking around Montreal for work. He was told that Gerald Potterton (a well-known director who made *The Railrodder* with Buster Keaton in the 1960s) was looking for staff for a feature film called *Heavy Metal.* "Gerry was impressed with the fact I just happened to have the entire collection of *Heavy Metal* magazines and I was completely familiar with the artists, stories, and illustration styles of the magazine," recalls Gilland.

As it turns out, there was only one other artist working at the studio. It happened to be Gilland's artistic hero, Ryan Larkin. "Gerry asked me if I would be interested in working with Larkin on a storyboard he was doing for the *Heavy Metal* movie, for a segment of the film Ryan was going to direct. I was too excited to even react. In my world, Ryan was the most important animation filmmaker alive."

Gilland was then sent to Larkin's house to meet his idol. "There I was at Ryan's house, and he was just a very sweet, extremely gentle little guy, who put me at ease from the very first moment. There was no pretension in his manner or his tone, he addressed me as a fellow artist, and he seemed as humble as can be."

Gilland and Larkin were working on a story from *Heavy Metal* called "Shells." In it, a young couple, living in a post-apocalyptic wasteland, decide to take off their shells to make love. However, once naked, they are devoured by a swarm of insects.

During the next few months, Gilland was giddy over the experience of working with Larkin:

> *I learned more about drawing, storyboarding, storytelling, and filmmaking than I had in the previous five years. Ryan opened me up to a whole new way of seeing and thinking. His imagination was powerful and dynamic, and constantly shifting with ideas, firing off too fast for me to keep up with them.*
>
> *Ryan constantly tripped over his words, as if his brain was going faster than his tongue, and I was a captive and willing audience, eyes and ears opened. I was only 22 years old, Ryan was 14 years older than me, and I always felt I was in the company of a genius, albeit a madman of sorts, too.*
>
> *But, if there was one thing I had learned in art school, it was to pay attention, and be ready when teachers and lessons appear. I was a captive student to Ryan, always enthusiastic, excited, and at full attention, and this seemed to fire him up as well.*

Gilland and Larkin grew closer. In Larkin, Gilland found not only a mentor, but someone who shared his own doubts, fears and dreams about the world. “The wicked ways of the world shocked and baffled us,” recalls Gilland, “and we were both prone to seeking refuge in various forms of highly imaginative escapism. Unfortunately, the escape mechanisms of alcohol and drugs were all too accessible, and it was a bit of a problem from the get-go.”

Gilland had been warned about Larkin’s alcohol problem, but it was a world that he knew intimately. “I came from a world filled with people who liked drinking early in the day, and I wasn’t exempt from the temptation myself, although I was being a little more cautious than Ryan at the time.”

Ryan’s girlfriend Jean would ask Gilland to make sure that Ryan didn’t have any beer in the mornings. Gilland tried to steer Larkin away, but how can you expect a wide-eyed youth to start dictating the dos and don’ts of the world to someone he admires?

“Early in the afternoon, Ryan would broach the subject,” says Gilland, “and inevitably, I would be sent to the corner store to pick up some beer. I would sip cautiously, feeling guilty, and like there was too much at stake, but Ryan would get pretty buzzed, and frequently break into his angry rants about business and money. He had a frightening idea the world was out to get him, and the drink fueled it badly, and I could see he was trapped on a merry-go-round that wouldn’t let him get off.”

The partnership didn’t last. One morning Potterton called Gilland and told him that the *Heavy Metal* artists refused to given permission to have their story used for the film. Potterton had more work for Gilland, but Larkin wasn’t going to be kept around. “In retrospect,” recalls Gilland, “I think I was just too young to know how to go about addressing the situation to Ryan. I felt awkward, extremely disappointed, and confused. My hero, my teacher, my master, was being cast aside, and I was being handed a golden opportunity.”

Gilland stayed in touch with Larkin, but found it difficult to watch his increasingly erratic behaviour. "More often than not, he was angry, and full of venom," Gilland remembers. All his worst fears had been realized; 'they' were out to get him. 'They' didn't appreciate or understand him. He became increasingly manic in our conversations, and slowly we drifted apart."

After a brief period working on a variety of odd jobs, Larkin realized that his finances were out of whack. The gal he was sharing spit with was controlling his money and apparently ripping him off. "In the early '80s, I was getting angry with her, accusing her of stealing from me. She stole from me, took advantage of my weaknesses. Eventually I got thrown out 'cause I got thrown out. I lost everything. She took all my money. She got me in serious trouble with the government. I can't stand women. They're such horrible people."

Always a man with a good sense of humour, Larkin then adds a final complaint: "She wanted sex twice a night. I was having sex with my gentleman friend and had only so much to give."

At the same time, Larkin, admittedly without many options, gave up on the film industry: "I realized that even though I had made some good films, I was not a good filmmaker. I couldn't meet deadlines. Other people were pouring out bullshit. I was becoming disheartened with the whole process of films, I was getting paid a salary for junk films." So Larkin returned to his first love, being an artist.

For a short time, things were okay. Larkin fell in love with a man who put him up in a studio. "I did a lot of good paintings in the '80s. I moved all of my work down to this beautiful home. This lasted for about eight years, but he finally wanted to get rid of me. I'm very attractive, but evidently, I'm undesirable after awhile."

The 1990s found Larkin, now coke-free, starting over again on his own. His generosity with people resulted in a variety of folks taking advantage of his home. Friends in need of a fix stole paintings, drawings and sculptures. Virtually all of his art was pawned for dope, tricks or whatever was needed to survive. Eventually penniless and alone, Larkin was tossed out of his home. He lived on the streets of Montreal briefly before moving into the Old Brewery Mission. For years, all he kept with him was a few clothes, some books, and his little plastic pop bottle for beer.

To survive, Larkin took up panhandling, a job he takes very seriously. "This is my second job," he says. "My first job is an artist. This job is to get spare change for a beer and a cigarette."

Larkin is also very philosophical about his approach to his work:

"A panhandler on the street has what I think is two choices of how to make money. One is you can be miserable, dirty, hairy, looking like a crippled person. Another one is to perform with elaboration of gestures, just to try to make people interested. When I was working in front of Schwartz's the owner really liked me because I don't look like a horrible, miserable bum. I'm more or less dressed up and I look good and I present myself in a certain fashion, without self-pity and all those things. I never ask for money. What I say is (right arm extended), 'Bienvenue and bonne appetit.' I am a doorman. I always make sure I've got clean shirts and I don't smell too much. I just sorta prance and mince around, not so much as a big performance, just as a polite person. I can make $10-20 in two hours. I don't pay taxes. I don't pay the government. I don't pay union dues. This is take-home pay."

As for his family, Larkin rarely sees them anymore. "They kind of don't like me and consider me to be a failure and disappointment. [My brother Roger] doesn't like me either. I'm the black sheep. They worried about me being a security risk. They were paranoid about being robbed and murdered. So my mom called Roger and said they didn't want me to come there anymore. Roger came down and said, ‘Ryan, your parents are in their eighties and you can’t hang out here anymore. It’s still their house. It’s best that you stay away.’ Which is fine by me anyway, ’cause I’m a city kid and can’t stand the suburbs.”

When Larkin looks back on his life, he admits that he’s made more than a few mistakes. “I think too much and don’t act. I’m poor with spontaneity, even though I can dance and things like that. It occurs to me that I don’t make mistakes, I make blunders. I stumble onto something that I didn’t know was gonna happen, or the consequences of it. I was experimenting. I was making mistakes, but I couldn’t figure the mistakes except a couple of years later. I think making mistakes is a good idea because only by making mistakes can you be experimental in your endeavours.”

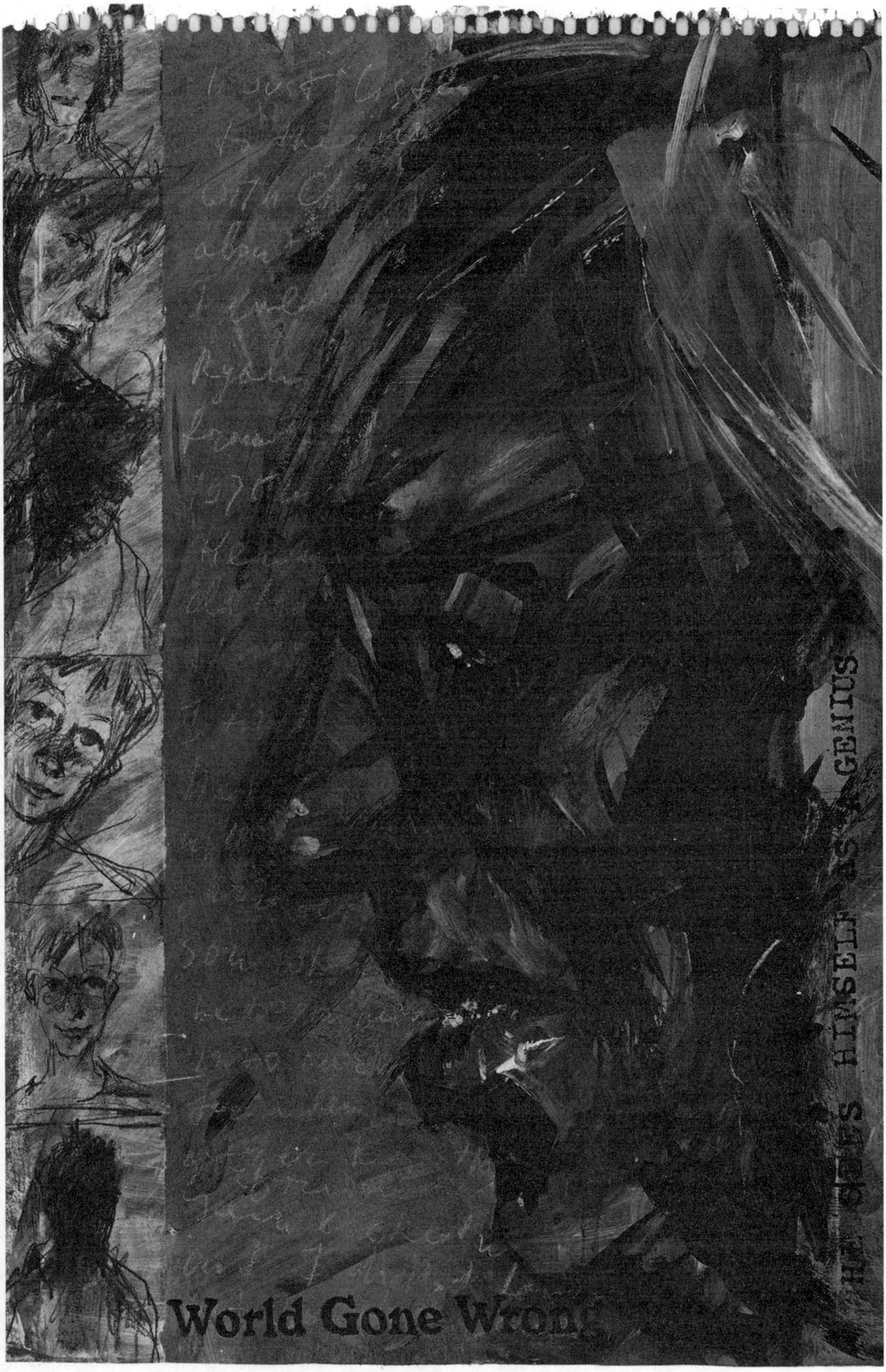
World Gone Wrong
HE SEES HIMSELF AS A GENIUS

he fear and confusion

later go

scinating I fear this

In November 2004, *Ryan* was nominated for an Academy Award® (it would eventually win).

A month later, Kelly forwarded me an email. It had been sent to her, Chris Landreth and CBC radio:

I just listened to the interview with Chris Landreth about his film "Ryan." I knew Ryan Larkin from 1975 to 1994. He was an old friend of my first husband. I find any sympathy for Ryan misplaced. Where is the sympathy for the children Ryan molested? He molested my 4-year-old son when we took him into our home for a few months after his then girlfriend Jean kicked him out. I did not find out about his pedophilia until my son was fifteen and confided his fears to his first girlfriend. Obviously Ryan had scared him sufficiently to keep his secret from us. [Note Ryan's anger in that scene about his drinking (I saw this often)]. Ryan has an enormous ego and a streak of, dare I say, "evil" that erases any conscience from his being. He sees himself as a genius, so no rules apply to him. Many people at the NFB saw the large mural of the naked young man with an erection that Ryan painted on the wall in the lobby and was then was asked to paint over. His attraction to young boys was excused as a part of his homosexuality and eccentricity. The boys we knew about were usually in their mid-teens and estranged from their families. I never thought he would touch a young child--but he did and the fear and confusion he instilled in my son effects him to this day. Ryan later got involved with a Black Magic group called the O.T.O (Aleister Crowley-"Do what thou wilt be the whole law"). Why did the filmmaker not interview Allan Macdonald who took Ryan in a short time after we kicked him out? We were too tolerant of his addictions and being surrounded by other artists with big egos we excused his debauchery because of his talent.

Talent is fascinating. I fear this film will just add to this fascination where it should be a warning to everyone to beware of egos who think the world owes them a living and they are too special to care about the harm they do to others.

The first of the deadly sins is pride. This is because it does not allow a person to see any of their faults and weaknesses and so they continue to cause pain to the people around them and blame others for their failings.

Please do not use my name. My son does not want to go public with his shame.

Why was she sending us this letter? What was I supposed to do with this accusation? If Ryan really did abuse this woman's son, then she should get a lawyer and press charges. Why tell me, Landreth, and all of Canada? Then again, maybe she felt that Ryan's life on the street was punishment enough. She probably figured he'd just die in obscurity on the streets. The sudden attention that Ryan was getting because of the film must have infuriated her.

Or maybe she was just another wing nut.

Oddly enough, a few months earlier a friend of mine had been busted for talking dirty to a 13-year-old on the Internet. Turned out that it wasn't a 13-year-old, but an undercover FBI agent. My friend had no previous charges and had never, apparently, done anything like this before. The friend was an intelligent guy, a teacher, and he'd never had any problems of this sort. I knew that he had problems at home, that his wife couldn't have children. The sad part of the story is that, just after he got arrested, his wife became pregnant (she'd had surgery to correct things). I truly believed that my friend had just made one big fuck-up. I don't believe he is/was a pedophile. But he committed the wrong crime in the wrong country at the wrong time. He'd have been better off committing a murder. At least he could get off on second-degree or manslaughter. So, in the end, my friend gets five years for talking dirty to an undercover officer. The penalty seemed harsh. As a mutual friend of ours wrote me, "If they really want to punish him, they should make him hang out with a 13-year-old for a year. That would be a real punishment."

Don't get me wrong, my pal fucked up. Whatever the excuses, circumstances, or truth, unless you got a nut for a brain, ya gotta know that dirty talk with a 13-year-old is just a no-go

All this talk about sex reminds me of Not Really My Pops and all that porno stuff that he stored in the basement. His forte at the police department was pedophiles and Internet crime. Why on earth was he bringing this stuff home? It wasn't that the porn was so alarming. I'd been having sex since I was 15, and besides, our house was always full of porn magazines that Not Really My Pops kept under his bed. That's how I learned about sex. So here's a guy with an obvious taste for pornography (a passion I share on occasion), a guy who was a lousy father and who ended up basically bailing on his sons, who was now out there protecting the world's children. It was a damn fine piece of irony. Was it guilt? Was it intrigue? He scared me because he seemed so fucking sure about the world. It was all neatly divided in his mind. It was such a crock. How could a guy who was as gray and "immoral" as anyone else actually believe that good and bad were so easily divided? He didn't care about motivations. Perps were just sick people who needed to be gotten rid of. He refused to see the bigger picture 'cause in his mind there was no bigger picture.

Part of that lived in me. I hated myself and Not Really My Pops for it. I wanted to bust Ryan when I heard this news. But why? It was just the word of a stranger. Maybe she was nuts. Maybe she was spurned by Ryan decades ago. Who the hell knew?

In the end, I said nothing — except to close friends. Not that it mattered. The letter had been sent out to others, including our national radio broadcaster. Besides, my dislike of Ryan was my own. It had nothing to do with any letters. I just didn't like him as a person, period. He'd given up on life and was content to exploit everyone around him. In a sense, he was the boy who never grew up: a gifted child who was used to having things go his way. His success came fast. He was too young to handle it.

Every month or so I read or hear about someone else who wants to save Ryan. One day this guy who worked downstairs in our building came up and started talking to my colleague. He talked excitedly about how he and a friend had made a pilgrimage to meet Ryan. They drank beers with him and went back to a friend's place to drink some more. Then the guy's tone changed. I could feel like he wanted to say something, but didn't have the nerve. My colleague pointed out that I'd been the guy who "found" Ryan. The guy was pleased and asked me about him.

"I think Larkin is an asshole. He's just mooching off people. The guy was no fucking genius either."

The guy was relieved. He told me about the racist comments that Larkin made and the many stupid things he said. "I started to feel really uncomfortable around him and wanted to get out, but my friend was so smitten with him."

"Yeah… sorry to hear that… but that's Ryan."

"Man, it's such a relief to hear that. I thought maybe I was being crazy, and I didn't want to say anything 'cause everyone is in love with this guy."

A few weeks later I learned about a website that had been created for Ryan. The authors wrote about how he was hard at work on storyboarding his next film. They set up a PayPal account so people could donate. I wondered where all the prize money had gone. I figured he'd made at least $10,000. Surely that would be enough to help him start his film. But there wouldn't be a film. Ryan had been storyboarding this film for at least two years now. Every time I spoke to either him or Chris, he was storyboarding. Maybe these people were genuine. Like me, like others, they really believed they were gonna save Ryan.

I guess what left me angry is that I felt betrayed in a way. I really felt like I'd connected with him, that he was a friend, that what we had done meant something to him. In the end, I'm not so sure. I think we were just a few more faces in one long compartment of a string of anonymous train cars travelling in and out of the life of Ryan Larkin.

Yet, Ryan somehow made us feel special. He inadvertently led me along the path to sobriety and gave me a pile of writing material as I tried to figure it all out. Whatever the problems with Landreth's film, meeting Ryan lit a fire under Chris and gave his life a direction. Maybe he didn't really come to terms with himself or his mother's death, but he made a film that people loved and suddenly he was hot shit. The weirdest irony was that one of the producers of the film was the National Film Board, the very studio that inadvertently created the monster. *Ryan* was their biggest success in years and they milked its success to the fullest. The studio that some felt had betrayed Ryan (although that was questionable) now found itself back on the international map, thanks to the film. Everyone Ryan touched seemed to be affected, for better or worse. Ryan stood as an image of the one road we could all take; a road of irresponsibility, of hopelessness, of resignation. He gave up on life. He gave up on himself. It's one thing to make it all heroic and say that he turned his back on society, but he didn't. He still sucked from its teats daily. He gladly accepted welfare cheques, never turned down a dime from anyone, drank beer and smoked.

It's a strange situation. Lesya and I tried to lift Ryan out of the water, but in the end, I wonder if we didn't end up taking him to a lower depth. Between 2000 and 2004, he slowly ascended into both the national and animation spotlight. Before then he lived in relative obscurity with his small group of friends and the momentary exchange with a passer-by on the street. Ryan didn't like fame the first time around and I wondered if all the new attention was bringing him to a place worse than the one he occupied when we first met him.

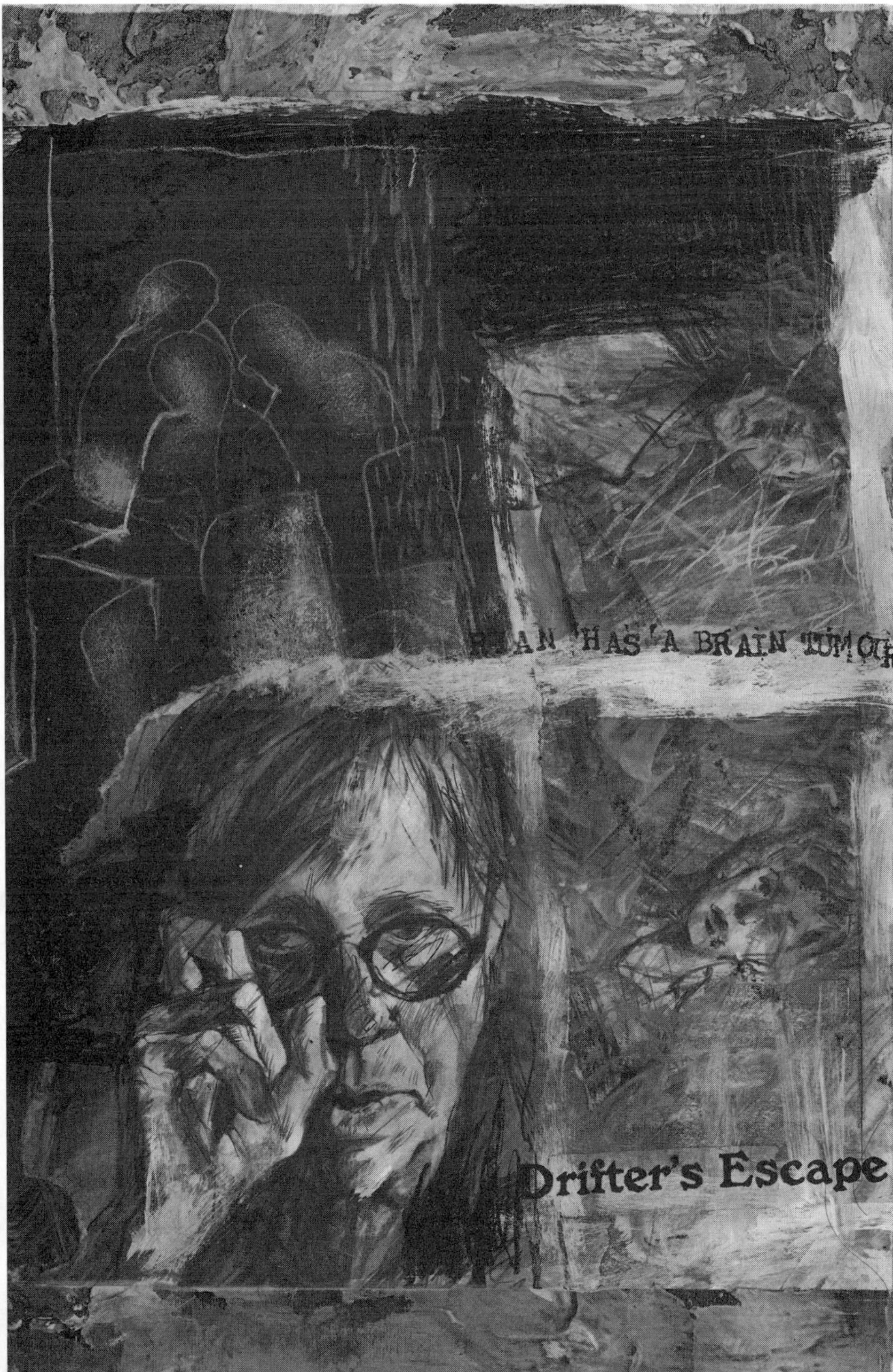
HAS A BRAIN TUMOUR
Drifter's Escape

k of a better word,
Lipsett
mother
hem
didn't w
psett rem

"Ryan has a brain tumour," Michele Cournoyer said to me as we sat in an Italian cafe in Montreal.

"What? Where did you hear this?"

"He had dinner with someone at the NFB recently."

I fell back into my chair, my mind starting to race nowhere in particular. I was in Montreal doing research for a film that I was working on with animator Theodore Ushev about another old dysfunctional NFB artist, Arthur Lipsett. On the surface the parallels were striking. Lipsett was a youngster when he joined the NFB, had a massive hit with his first film *Very Nice, Very Nice*, but then slowly descended into, for lack of a better word, madness. Eventually he killed himself. Like Larkin, Lipsett witnessed a tragedy as a child. When he was 10, he saw his mother take rat poison, leave the house and never come back. Initially, art provided Lipsett with an escape. He could find solace, comfort and purpose in films. Soon that wasn't enough. His films got increasingly more chaotic. Most people couldn't understand them. After he quit the NFB, he began showing signs of depression, eccentric behaviour (he was perhaps autistic), and he couldn't and maybe didn't want to climb out of the darkness. But through it all, Lipsett remained a person people liked. He didn't inflict his pain on others. In the end, his suicide was perhaps done to spare his friends and family.

Unlike Lipsett, Ryan played off the fragile, broken boy routine to elicit sympathy. There was always someone to come running. I wasn't the first, nor was I the last. But since that letter reached me in 2004, I carried a lot of pain and confusion. I didn't save Ryan, but if I didn't make that trip to Montreal to meet him and invite him back to Ottawa, then none of this resurrection stuff would have happened. He would not have met Chris Landreth. There would have been no film, no awards, no minor fame. No pilgrimages by youngsters to meet the second coming of Christ. If I hadn't gone there that day, because I was desperately sad, lonely and angry about Biopops' rejection and needed to find someone to save my sorry ass, then Ryan Larkin would have stayed dead and buried on St. Laurent St.

Before I left to get my train home, I told Theo and Michele that I had to go see Ryan, that I had to show him the letter.

* * *

A few nights later I'm watching *Capote*, a movie about Truman Capote writing his classic nonfiction book *In Cold Blood*. The book was based on a true story about the murder of a Kansas family. What was intriguing about Capote's book was his humane portrait of the killers. He visited them and got to know them and even hired lawyers to appeal their death sentence. He did it solely because he wanted to keep them alive until they gave him a detailed description of the murders. He couldn't finish the book without this story. When he finally got what he needed, he finished his book and stopped hiring lawyers to help them. The men were finally put to death and Capote had a bestseller. However, his life was never the same. Consumed by guilt, he never wrote another book and let alcohol take his pain away until he died.

Why did we get this film now? We subscribe to a mail-order movie service, so the choice was somewhat random. Still, not to romanticize it too much, I saw the parallels and felt even more sure that I had to confront Larkin about the allegations. And, yes, like Capote, I knew that, more than anything, this turn of events was giving me closure for this book.

The next day, I confirmed the story that Larkin did have cancer. In fact, I was told that as a result of the radiation treatment, he'd also developed a brain tumour. Those who saw him said he looked decent enough, had put on weight, and wasn't drinking. He wasn't living at the Old Brewery Mission anymore either. He was being cared for by a woman named Laurie, whom he'd likely encountered on St. Laurent Street over the years. She was a young, peppy musician with a good heart. Knowing that Ryan was ill, she took him into her home in St. Hyacinthe, a small town about 45 minutes east of Montreal. I was always doubtful about Ryan's saviours, especially since the film. Not that I mistrusted Laurie, but maybe she naively thought she could help him too. Then again, maybe this was different. This was mortality he was now facing. To her credit, Laurie got Ryan off the streets. He was in a nice, quiet home away from downtown temptation. For years he spoke of making a new film called *Spare Change*. Laurie encouraged and gently pushed him and, as a result, he received a Canada Council arts grant for the film and had done a rough storyboard. I was still doubtful about it and wondered what she was getting out of it, but we'd all gotten something out of Ryan.

I rang Laurie up. She knew who I was and had read my articles on Ryan. I explained that I wanted to come and meet him. She said it was no problem, but just to call in advance to ensure that someone was home. This worried me a bit. I wanted to meet Ryan one-on-one, not with a keeper around. Then again, this was her house and I was pretty much a stranger. Laurie assured me that Ryan was in good health and she was optimistic that he'd live long. She also admitted that she's a naturally optimistic person, even when reality tells her otherwise.

I wasn't so optimistic. Ryan might look good today, but tomorrow he could slip fast. I knew that I had to see him now, so I made plans to rent a car and drive to St. Hyacinthe to see him the next week... for the last time.

Of course, it didn't end there. For the next week, I wavered back and forth about going. Why was I doing this? Yes, it was for this book. Selfish? Yep. I mean, who the fuck was I to confront him?

I'm no angel, saint or saviour. Let's assume he did the deed. So what? It's the victim's problem. Besides, if he is dying, isn't that his punishment? Yes, he had all this fame from this film and some arts council money, but so what? He's still without a home, without a life. Once the film was finished, everyone slowly forgot about Ryan. So, fuck it, let him die alone. Did I really expect him to tell me anything? He didn't owe me a thing. So what the fuck was this all about? Am I not reverting back to this "seeking a saviour" business again? Am I really expecting closure again?

The drive was uneventful. My son Jarvis and I had just gone to see Dylan two nights earlier. I brought some of his CDs along for the drive. Just me, Bob and the road. I put in *Highway 61* and was struck by the lines in "Like a Rolling Stone":

> Once upon a time you dressed so fine
> You threw the bums a dime in your prime, didn't you?
> People'd call, say, "Beware doll, you're bound to fall"
> You thought they were all kiddin' you
> You used to laugh about
> Everybody that was hangin' out
> Now you don't talk so loud
> Now you don't seem so proud
> About having to be scrounging for your next meal.
>
> How does it feel
> How does it feel
> To be without a home
> Like a complete unknown…

Was Ryan the doll bound to fall?

Was I the lost, naive Mr. Jones of another Dylan song on the album, *Ballad of a Thin Man*? Not sure of what he would find, let alone what he was seeking?

Then along came thoughts of the *Gospel of Thomas*: "Let he who seeks not stop seeking until one finds. When one finds, one will be troubled. When one is troubled, one will marvel and will reign over all."

I was troubled and I guess that was good.

Paranoid thoughts. Probably fuelled by the bizarre murder of actress Adrienne Shelly, I get it into my head that maybe Laurie and Ryan know why I'm coming. Are they gonna kill me? Make sure you don't take any drinks or food from them. I even stop to get a coffee before I arrive, just so I can beg off when they offer a drink.

I arrive.

Laurie is there with her toy dog to greet me. She's living in this massive old house. It's about 140 years old, she tells me. It's huge. It's not quite the Eastman mansion, but still, there's gotta be about a dozen rooms. She takes me on a tour. My nerves calm. She's a good person. Clearly, she's got a lot of space and can afford to have Ryan there without him really getting in the way of her life. She ends the tour with Ryan's room. There he is lying on the bed. The room is small and somehow it seems not that different from a room he might stay in at the Brewery Mission.

He rises from the bed, puts his glasses on. I say hello and we shake hands. His hands look ragged and fragile, almost skeletal. Otherwise, he looks relatively okay. He's put on a little bit of weight and doesn't appear to be shaking anymore. He tells me that he had to give up beer because of the radiation treatments. Apparently the two didn't go well together. He's pissed off about it, but said that too often he was passing out in the streets even though he wasn't drunk. I look around the small room. There's a poster he's done for a festival in Montreal, a microwave, lots of drawings on the wall, and an old animation table from the NFB. Laurie tells me that they gave it to him as a gift last Xmas. Scattered on the table are some pencil drawings, and on a bulletin board nearby I see what appear to be storyboard sketches for the *Spare Change* film. It's the most I've ever seen from an idea that I'd heard about since I first met Ryan.

Laurie grabs me a chair and I take a seat. She offers me a coffee. I say yes without thinking about my earlier fears of being poisoned.

First things first. I hand Ryan a copy of my *Unsung Heroes of Animation* book. He was among the animators I wrote about in this book and I figured it was a good way to break the ice and keep things calm. (It's also a fine bit of product placement.) He accepts the book and actually seems a bit excited. He skims through, checking out the pictures and names.

I notice that a cat and dog sit snugly on Ryan's bed. The dog, the same little toy dog I met when I arrived, is sitting next to him. In such a big house, these two animals clearly find comfort with Ryan. Although I can't tell if the dog feels safe with Ryan or is protecting him.

For the next hour we shoot the shit, talking about cancer, the festival, living away from Montreal. I laugh when he tells me, "I still keep my room at the mission for my visits to Montreal." I wonder if someone is watching his panhandling spot for him too.

Ryan doesn't really seem to know what his health status is or if the cancer is gone. "The doctors don't really tell me anything." I wonder if that means that things probably aren't good. He says he's got some more tests/visits scheduled, so maybe he'll get a clear picture then.

I see a handful of rough scenes from *Spare Change* on the wall, along with a mess of drawings, but they just seem like a lot of fragments. I don't get a sense of where he's going with this. There's a story here. Who else could tell an authentic tale about living on the street? In truth, all of his films are rather scatterbrained and nonlinear. They reflect the mind of someone damaged, someone without consistent focus. I can empathize with that. Most artists probably can, but still, it's frustrating for me to watch him taking his time in the face of death. Then again, I guess we all do.

Maybe it's not important that he finishes the film. Perhaps just spending his last days working on something positive, excavating his years living on the street, is tonic enough.

Laurie comes in to say that she's heading out to the hardware store. She offers to get Ryan some protein shakes. He doesn't eat much, so he needs these Boost drinks to supplement his diet. To my surprise, he pulls out a roll of $20 bills to cover the cost of a six-pack of the stuff. He's got more money than I do. I suspect it's the Canada Council grant or maybe some of his money from Chris's movie. As soon as I hear Laurie's car pull out, I decide that this is the time.

I pull out the letters and tell Ryan I need to broach a rather unpleasant subject. "I've been carrying this stuff for two years now and I think it's time for you to see them." I hand him the letters and for the next five minutes or so he sits quietly on the bed reading. His face shows no reaction.

I was nervous. I really wanted to leave. I had no idea how he would react. Would he freak out? I wasn't worried that he'd harm me. He's a fluff of a fellow. But I didn't want a big commotion.

There was no need to worry. He finished the letter and, without knowing who had written it or really any specific details, he went on about how women used to try to blackmail him because he drew pictures of naked children. He said something about how they'd try and sell his art to make "hundreds of thousands of dollars." He really believed this. Of course, he also believed that George Lucas had ripped him off.

As Ryan speaks, I do my best to avoid looking at him. I shift my eyes to his animation table. Atop it sits a disturbing picture of Ryan from the 1970s. He's got long hair, lipstick, and he's standing inside a jukebox. It looks like he's alive inside a coffin.

Things suddenly get very awkward. I say that I'm not there to look for answers — which, yes, wasn't entirely true — and that I'm not here to judge him (I already had, hadn't I?), but that I had lived with this for two years, that as he was rising in the public eye, as people were salivating over him, eager to be around him, I was holding this disturbing accusation (one that I once said didn't mean a damn thing to me).

I wonder who was more pathetic and parasitic? Did I care about the alleged victim? I didn't even know his name. I just wanted a good story to give my life some edge and purpose. When I couldn't get my mother or fathers to take responsibility, to acknowledge my pains, I guess I figured Ryan would, that he'd acknowledge his guilt, that he'd finally confront himself. His answers caught me off guard. He assured me that he wasn't a sex menace, but then said that people didn't understand his eccentricities and that boys need men to learn about the world. He admitted that he was worried when he started getting attention for Landreth's film because he thought that people from the past would come out trying to blackmail him again.

He gets up to go the washroom. He takes a long time. My head spins paranoid tunes. I expect to hear a gunshot, or maybe he'll come back and try to stab or shoot me. Fuck. I just want to get out of here. I've said what I needed to say, now I just want to flee.

One of the storyboard sketches catches my eye. The scene has Ryan — with long hair and beard — standing at the gates of Heaven. He has moved here because it's a good spot to make money. St. Peter sees Ryan and tells him that he has to move along, that this is his spot. "Well, where am I supposed to go?" asks Ryan.

"Let me show you the way. You go down to the end of this street, take a left and keep going till you reach hell. That's where you should be."

It was actually a funny scene and, while I'm not sure Ryan saw it as anything more than a good joke, the scene certainly resonated with me.

When Ryan returned to the room, he had no gun or knife. Just took a long dump, I guess. Probably those protein shakes. Filled with crap.

I told him I'd better hit the road. He thanked me for coming and seemed to mean it. I could never tell with him. Sometimes I wonder if he even really knows who I am. Certainly, given the blackouts he's had because of the tumours, I'm surprised he remembers me at all. Before I leave, I promise him I'll send over a copy of the Lipsett documentary that he's interviewed in. But it's all small talk. I just want to leave. In a sense, this "confrontation" has been anticlimatic. You look at him and see a fractured, pathetic little thing and just think, "Fuck, his existence is his suffering."

Before I leave, we shake hands. I'm careful grabbing his hand. The fingers look like they'll snap off with the slightest pressure. As I walked out the door, I looked at him and said, "Well, good luck with everything. I hope that things turn out as they should."

That was it. That was all.

I pulled out of the driveway and drove a bit. I felt nauseous. What had I done? Once on the street, I pulled the car to the side and held my stomach for a few minutes.

Then I went home.

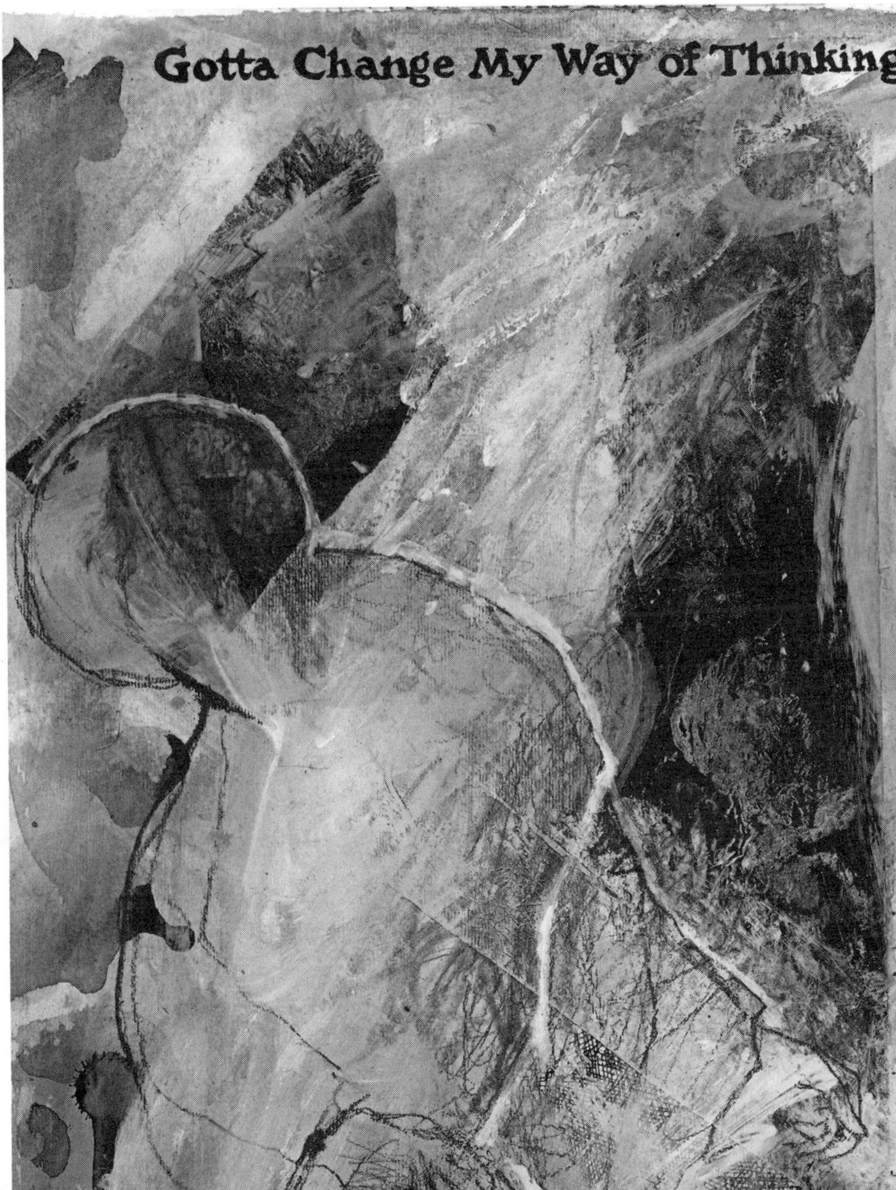
Gotta Change My Way of Thinking
THE GOD WE NEVER KNEW

was a bi sed beca
viewe ple
ome
is tradition
urches
ous festivals and
Durir

Recently, I started having conversations with a friend of mine named Don. I'm not really sure how we met. He was a lecturer when I took film studies at university, but I'd never had him for a teacher. We connected initially because of a shared passion for film noir. Don had a slew of rare noirs that he shared with me. He's also just a heck of a fascinating and smart guy. Hanging out with him is like having a good meal for the brain and the soul. There's always something to learn.

A few years ago, I learned that he went to church and was into religious history. I was a bit surprised because he didn't seem like a religious type. (I viewed religious people as weak and desperate, without any sense of identity). Initially I didn't really ask a lot about Don's involvement with the church, but over time, I got this sense that he enjoyed the communal nature of it. You're there with other people, sharing songs and words and rituals. In a society where I felt that people had become increasingly alienated from one another, I was drawn to the spirit of his attraction. Besides, I'd always felt comfortable in churches. I'd visited many around the world while travelling to various festivals and I just started to feel this sense of shelter and solitude. It was calming. During those times I began to see animation festivals as a sort of chapel that brought our community together for a few days to share films, sing songs, drink, eat, fuck, and talk about our loves and lives. Animation has been a sanctuary, providing us with a space to find, cleanse, confess, define, lose and discover ourselves.

As I returned to this book in 2008, Don and I began to talk in more detail. I was really intrigued by the notion of the Jesus of faith vs. the Jesus of history. Don loaned me a few books and we talked about this conflict between faith and fact. I particularly enjoyed Marcus Borg's *The God We Never Knew*. In it the author asks: "Is the Christian life about believing in God as a supernatural being separate from the universe or about a relationship to the Spirit who is right here and all around us?"

For many of us, God is this guy who lives in heaven, takes requests, and acts as a sort of superego. Within this model, Borg argues that sin is the centre of existence and that we end up constantly trying to measure up to this superego. Invariably, you never do. Borg suggests that God should instead be looked upon as a spirit. The Hebrew word for "spirit," says Borg, is "ruach," which means "wind" and "breath." We can't see either, but they're both real. God now becomes something that is right here beside us. God was about connection, not sin.

Discovering God is about finding something you've lost. It's kind of like when you can't find your glasses and then discover that they're right there on your forehead.

Alongside the *Gospel of Thomas*, I found Borg's interpretation of God liberating. It wasn't that it suddenly made me want to embrace religion or believe in God. Instead, these views helped me get a grip on my own insecurities and fears. There was no reason to fear anymore and the words of Borg and Thomas went against everything I believed growing up; my childhood idea of God and his human stand-in, Not Really My Pops, was that they were intimidating and infallible bullies whose mandate was "do it my way or else."

* * *

In 2005, the Montreal weekly paper *Hour* interviewed Larkin in anticipation of *Ryan* being nominated for the Oscars*. I had given up reading articles about Ryan because they all said the same thing. In this case, the author met up with him, had some beers and shot the shit about the past, present and future. I stumbled upon the article in March 2008 in the National Film Board of Canada's archives. In it, I found a quote from Larkin that seemed to sum up his direction with great clarity and honesty:

> I make all these excuses for my behaviour, but the truth is, I was a lazy sonofabitch and I fucked up. In the end, I have to admit it. I had difficulty handling my ego when I was famous. I've made a fool of myself — during the '80s and '90s I was not functioning properly. Most articles say it was a drug problem, but it wasn't just that. It was a psychological problem I had to deal with, and my first choice was to use drugs. I had sexual proclivities, too — I was doing coke and getting hard-ons instead of what I should have been doing, which was making interesting, comical, beautiful animation films.

I'd intended to write a book that raged against Ryan and Biopops. I wanted the world to know what a fraud these people were for not taking responsibility for their lives, but after reading the passage above, a wave of sadness crashed over me. I immediately recognized and understood what Ryan was saying (okay, except for the coke stuff). Ryan suddenly seemed no different than me. I have left behind a long trail of harmful actions that I know hurt other people. I didn't think I was a bad person. I didn't consciously try to hurt people. I always felt deep regret and remorse. Yet, no matter how bad I felt, I'd turn around and screw up again. All the while, though, Kelly stood with me, always supportive, even when I turned against her and ridiculed her faith in me.

Faith requires strength. Landreth, Laurie and Kelly have it and I don't. However, instead of admitting my weakness, I've cloaked my admiration and envy behind a sheath of contempt. I became the very bully I feared my entire life.

Suddenly I remembered an incident that happened after I'd found a text about Biopops online. It had his photo and talked a bit about his education and background. I was really excited to find out these extra crumbs of information and immediately sent it to my friend Maral. Her response surprised me. "So what?" she wrote. "Do you feel great emotion when you look at his picture? Is there a connection? Does the image trigger memories or feelings?" In a second, she'd deflated me and slapped me into reality. I looked at the photo and realized that it meant nothing to me. It could have been anyone. There was nothing special about this guy and I certainly felt no connection to the image. I knew the facts about Biopops. I knew he was my biological father, but so what? After that there was nothing. There was no faith/belief to grab hold of because there was no history between us, no love. There was nothing.

Just then I realized that this was what Biopops had told me from the start.

* * *

After I finished my Larkin research at the NFB, I bumped into Michele Cournoyer in a corridor. In the midst of our conversation about the book, she suddenly asked, "Who are you trying to blame this time?" I was taken aback and angered by her comment. Now, though, I realize that she was right. I didn't really care if Ryan and Biopops lived or died. Trying to save Ryan and find Biopops was a ruse, another excuse to avoid taking responsibility for the here and now of my own mess of a life. I am the one who has not been taking responsibility for his life.

I couldn't believe in Ryan because I had no faith in myself.

I wanted to believe in Biopops for the very same reason.

It was too late now anyway. Ryan didn't need to be saved anymore.

Neither did I.

I never did.

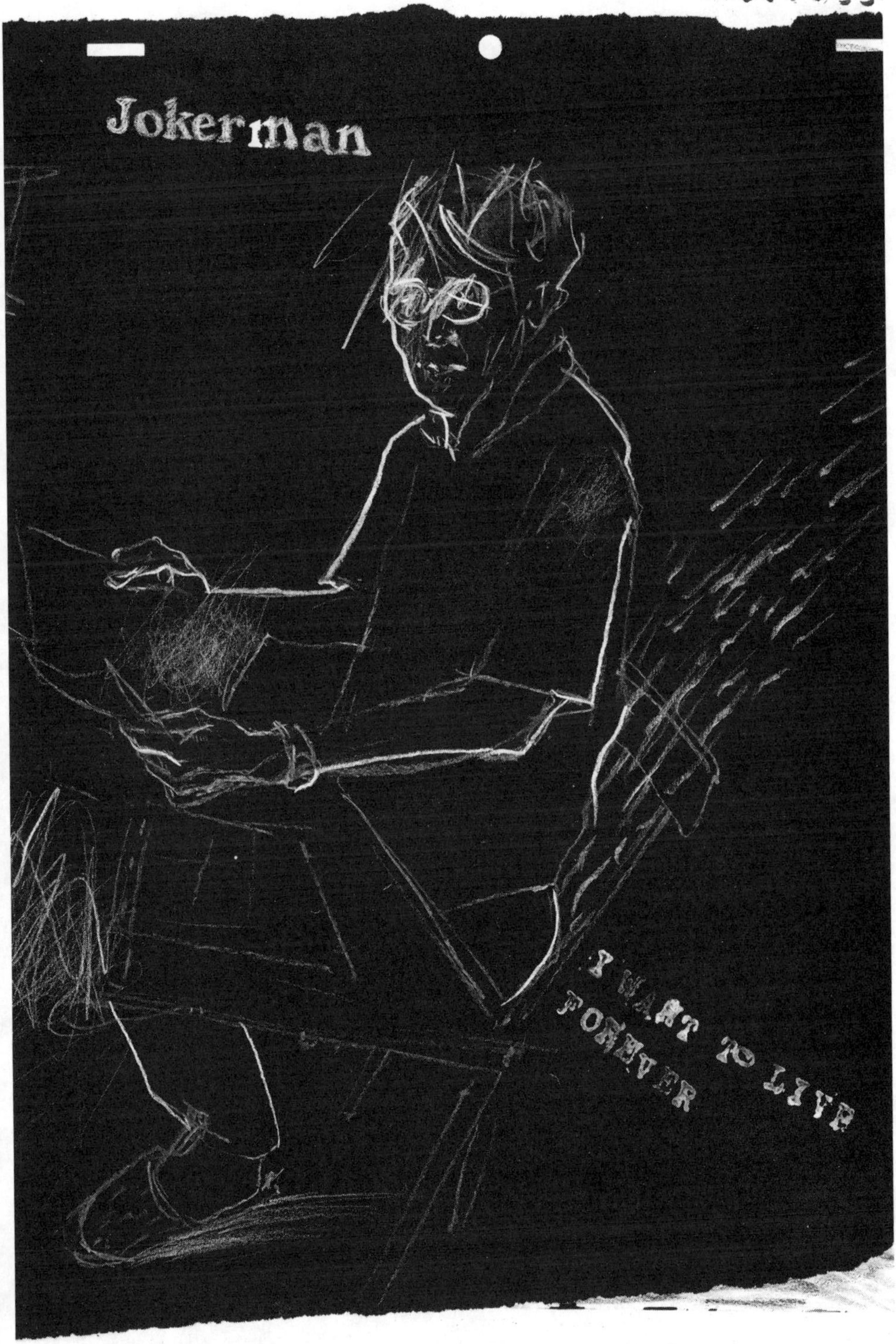
Jokerman
I WANT TO LIVE
FOREVER

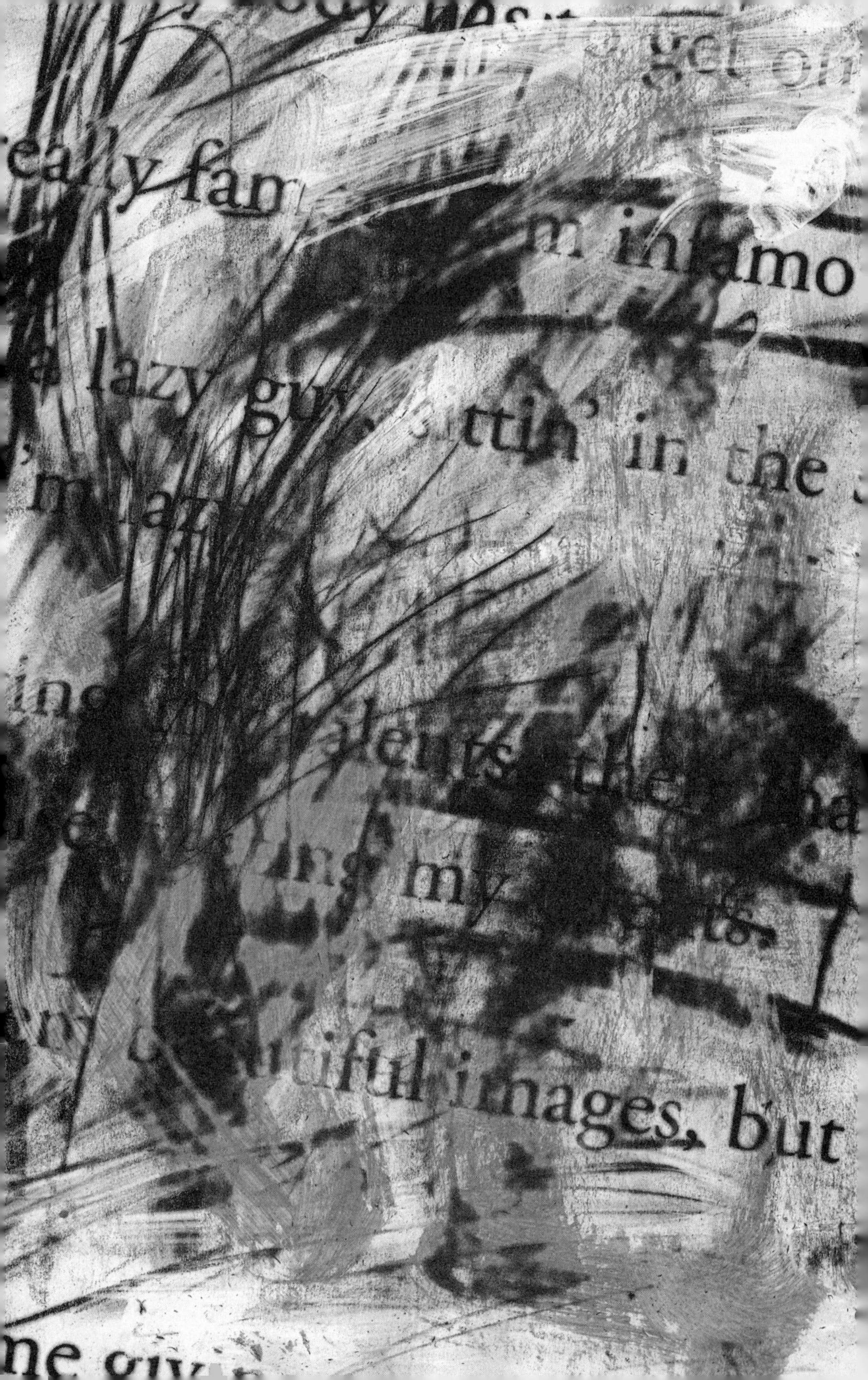
get on
eally fan
m infamo
a lazy guy
ttin' in the
my
images, but

No matter how bad things got, Ryan always maintained a pretty good sense of humour. In interviews and conversations, he occasionally blurted out some nifty one-liners that seemed like outtakes from the fragments of Heraclitus:

I'm still a rebellious teenager. I want to smoke a cigarette and have a beer and everybody has to get out of my way.

I'm not really famous. I'm infamous.

I was just a lazy guy, sittin' in the sun forever watching the birds in the trees. I'm lazy.

If I'm wasting my talents, then that's more important to me than somebody else wasting my talents.

I can give them beautiful images, but I cannot give them their peace of mind.

I don't think me giving up my personal habits is anything more than me wiping my ass. What's going to become of us? Are all of us people going to be examined right up to our assholes with fine computer chips shoved into our thighs?

What's in it for me?

I hate the Beatles.

I've been deprived.

I think I'm a dinosaur. I should jump off a cliff, but I'm afraid of heights.

I want to live forever, like everybody, if not in my body, in people's minds.

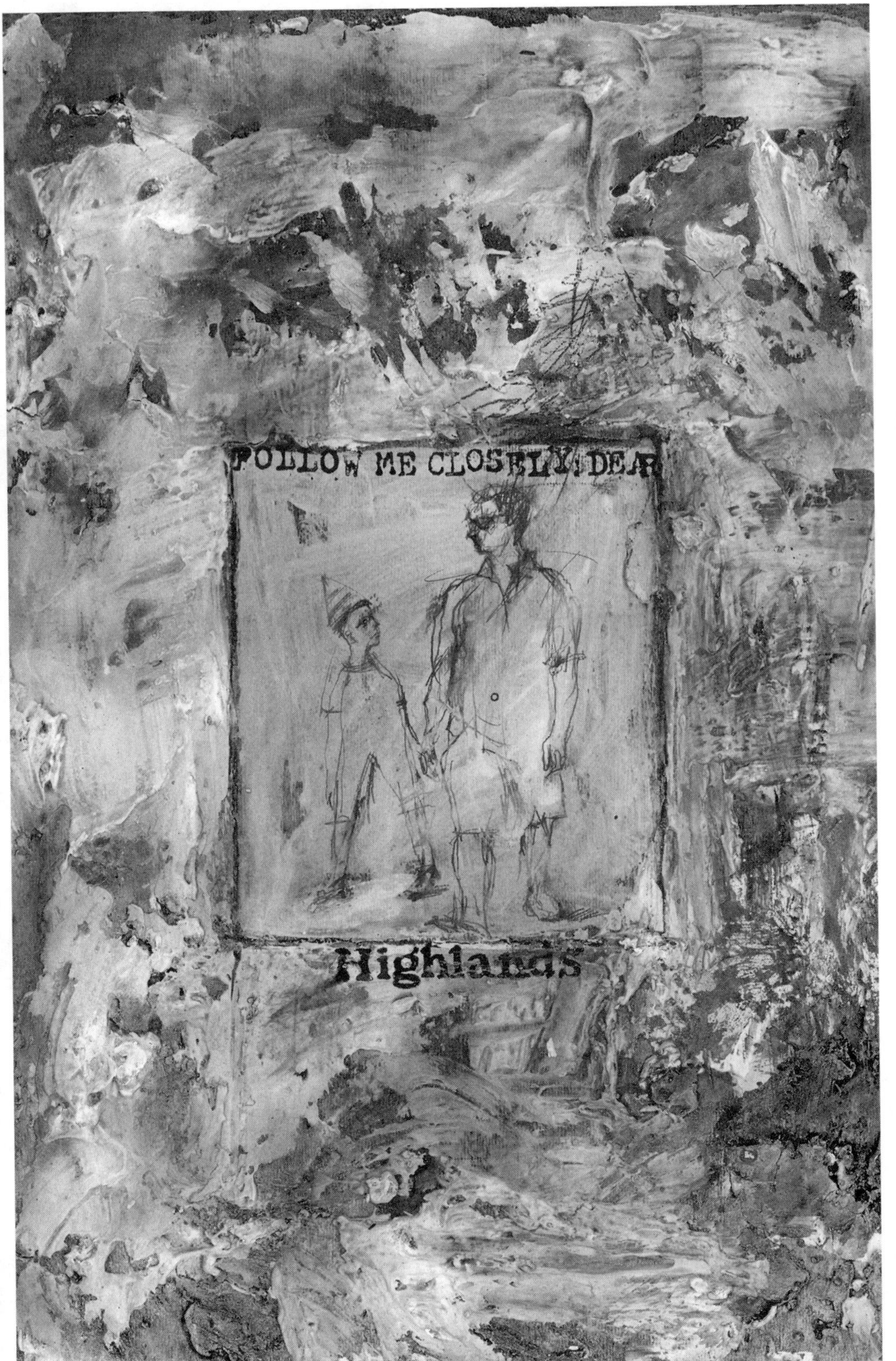
FOLLOW ME CLOSELY, DEAR
Highlands

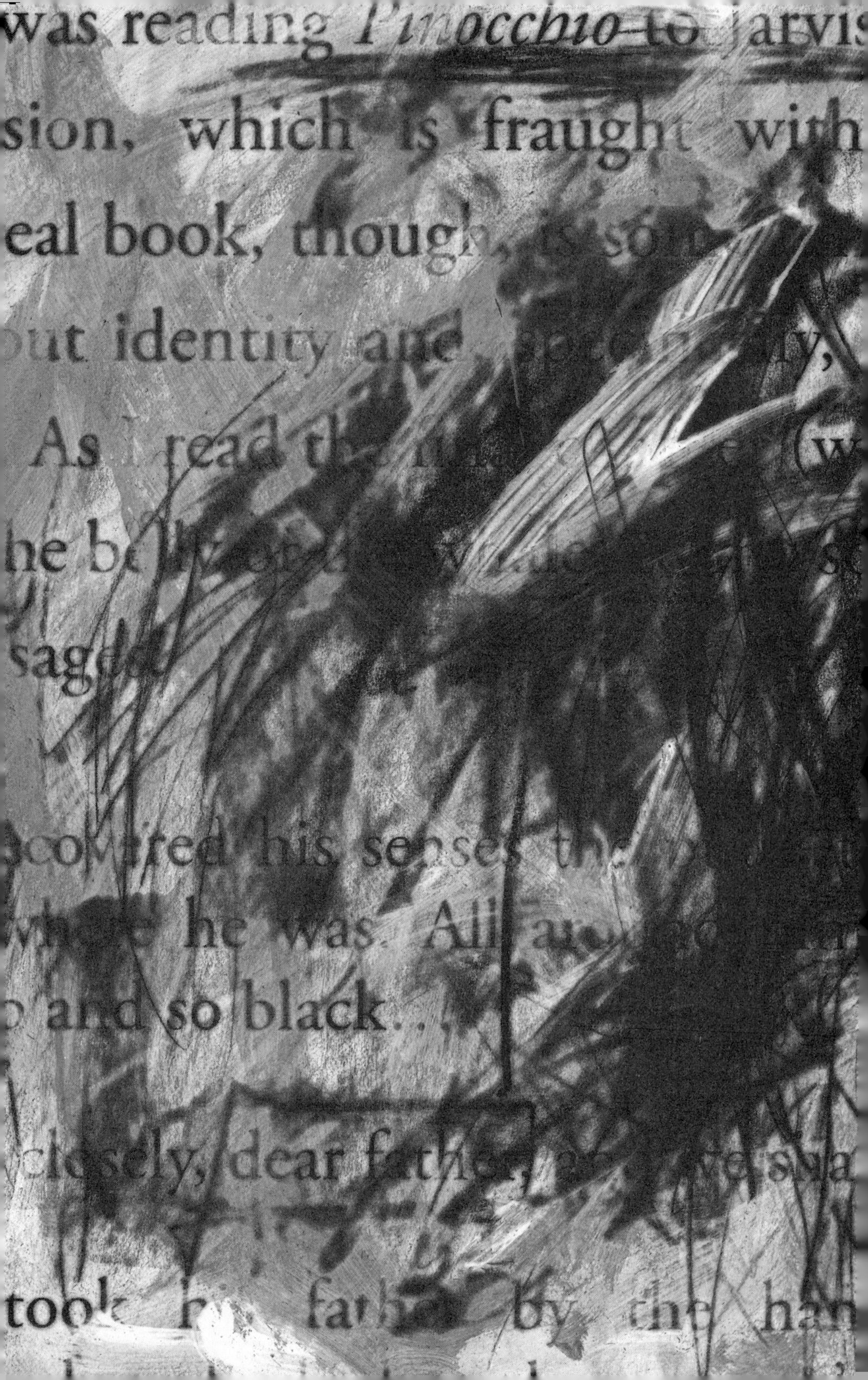
was reading Pinocchio
sion, which is fraught with
eal book, though
ut identity
As I read
his senses
he was. All
and so black.
closely, dear father
took father by the

Last night I was reading *Pinocchio* to Jarvis. I'd only ever known the Disney version, which is fraught with sanitized saccharine sweetness. The real book, though, is something totally different. It's a dark book about identity and, specifically, about boys and men, fathers and sons. As I read the final chapter (when Pinocchio rescues his father from the belly of the whale) to my son, I was struck by the power of the passages:

> When he recovered his senses the puppet could no longer remember where he was. All around him was darkness, a dark so deep and so black…
>
> "Follow me closely, dear father, and we shall soon be saved."
>
> Pinocchio took his father by the hand and, walking precariously, they climbed up the monster's throat…
>
> "Father, father, what has happened? Tell me, please!" cried Pinocchio, who ran to his father and embraced him tightly and kissed him with great affection.
>
> "You're the cause of all these sudden changes, my dear Pinocchio," answered Geppetto.

Did I get it all wrong? I kept looking for my father to save me, but perhaps it's the son who saves the father.

* * *

A few years back Jarvis and I were at the mall. Santa Claus was there. I asked him if he wanted to see Santa.

"No," he said.

"Why not?"

"I just don't want to."

"But he's right there. There's no line-up. This is your chance."

"Dad," he said, getting increasingly annoyed, "I don't want to. We can go tomorrow after my dentist appointment."

"Okay, but I don't understand. He's right there. Tomorrow there will be line-ups."

"Dad!!!"

"Okay. Fine. Another time."

We walked for another ten minutes and Jarvis suddenly turned and said, "Okay, I want to see Santa now."

I just laughed and said, "Sure."

He was shy as he approached Santa's chair, but gradually he relaxed and got into a conversation with the man in red. After a few minutes, he hopped off the chair and headed towards the exit.

As I stood waiting, he approached me bursting with happiness. He's usually very self-conscious, especially about smiling. It's almost as though he's afraid to just let go and smile. This time he couldn't help it. He was beaming with warmth and confidence.

"So, how was it?" I asked.

"Good," he said, returning to a guarded tone.

"Did you tell him what you wanted?"

"Yeah. He's the real Santa."

"How do you know?"

"I can tell. The beard isn't on a string. It's real. He has glasses too."

"Well, aren't you glad we came here then?"

"Yeah."

It was all so corny, but I couldn't help but smile. Seeing Jarvis's happiness triggered sensations I hadn't felt since I was a kid. It was like we were one for a second. He didn't need to explain. I got it. I felt it.

It wasn't about me believing in Santa Claus, it was about me believing in my son.

Acknowledgements

Lesya Fesiak, who opened the door.

Chris Landreth. We were travel partners on different roads. I owe Chris a huge amount of thanks. First, for his encouragement with this book. Secondly, for his friendship. Thirdly, for allowing me to use his 2001 video/audio interviews with Ryan. I had interviewed Ryan in 2000, but Chris's interviews enabled me to flesh out Ryan's life in more detail.

Jon Hofferman and Jen Noseworthy for editing and feedback.
Ron Diamond, Dan Sarto at Animation World Network.
Kevin Harreld at Cengage.

Theodore Ushev
Kelly, Jarvis, Betty, Harrison, Buster and Molly
Michele Cournoyer, Paul Fierlinger, Andreas Hykade
Andre and Pierre at the NFB Archives.
Madeleine Belisle for loaning me Larkin's films years ago.
AWN for permission to reprint Chris Landreth quotes.

Alyson Carty, Maral Mohammadian, Hayden Mindell, Andre Coutu, Signe Baumane, Dennis Tupicoff, George Griffin, David Ehrlich, Laurie Gordon, Christine Noel, Lisa Soper, Petr Mahr, Marcy Page (for giving the okay to use the Larkin/Landreth interviews), Michael Fukushima, David Verrall, Robert Verrall, Jarrett Zaroski, Azarin Sorabkhani, Amigo Tony, the guy who plays Bob Dylan, Don Wallace and finally, Santa Claus.

License Agreement/Notice of Limited Warranty

By opening the sealed disc container in this book, you agree to the following terms and conditions. If, upon reading the following license agreement and notice of limited warranty, you cannot agree to the terms and conditions set forth, return the unused book with unopened disc to the place where you purchased it for a refund.

License:
The enclosed software is copyrighted by the copyright holder(s) indicated on the software disc. You are licensed to copy the software onto a single computer for use by a single user and to a backup disc. You may not reproduce, make copies, or distribute copies or rent or lease the software in whole or in part, except with written permission of the copyright holder(s). You may transfer the enclosed disc only together with this license, and only if you destroy all other copies of the software and the transferee agrees to the terms of the license. You may not decompile, reverse assemble, or reverse engineer the software.

Notice of Limited Warranty:
The enclosed disc is warranted by Course Technology to be free of physical defects in materials and workmanship for a period of sixty (60) days from end user's purchase of the book/disc combination. During the sixty-day term of the limited warranty, Course Technology will provide a replacement disc upon the return of a defective disc.

Limited Liability:
THE SOLE REMEDY FOR BREACH OF THIS LIMITED WARRANTY SHALL CONSIST ENTIRELY OF REPLACEMENT OF THE DEFECTIVE DISC. IN NO EVENT SHALL COURSE TECHNOLOGY OR THE AUTHOR BE LIABLE FOR ANY OTHER DAMAGES, INCLUDING LOSS OR CORRUPTION OF DATA, CHANGES IN THE FUNCTIONAL CHARACTERISTICS OF THE HARDWARE OR OPERATING SYSTEM, DELETERIOUS INTERACTION WITH OTHER SOFTWARE, OR ANY OTHER SPECIAL, INCIDENTAL, OR CONSEQUENTIAL DAMAGES THAT MAY ARISE, EVEN IF COURSE TECHNOLOGY AND/OR THE AUTHOR HAS PREVIOUSLY BEEN NOTIFIED THAT THE POSSIBILITY OF SUCH DAMAGES EXISTS.

Disclaimer of Warranties:
COURSE TECHNOLOGY AND THE AUTHOR SPECIFICALLY DISCLAIM ANY AND ALL OTHER WARRANTIES, EITHER EXPRESS OR IMPLIED, INCLUDING WARRANTIES OF MERCHANTABILITY, SUITABILITY TO A PARTICULAR TASK OR PURPOSE, OR FREEDOM FROM ERRORS. SOME STATES DO NOT ALLOW FOR EXCLUSION OF IMPLIED WARRANTIES OR LIMITATION OF INCIDENTAL OR CONSEQUENTIAL DAMAGES, SO THESE LIMITATIONS MIGHT NOT APPLY TO YOU.

Other:
This Agreement is governed by the laws of the State of Massachusetts without regard to choice of law principles. The United Convention of Contracts for the International Sale of Goods is specifically disclaimed. This Agreement constitutes the entire agreement between you and Course Technology regarding use of the software.